Praise for *Strategies for Learning: Empowering Students for Success, Grades 9–12*

"*Strategies for Learning* contains proven practical and explicit strategies that secondary students with learning disabilities can use to become independent and motivated learners. Wedding years of clinical experience with the most up-to-date research, Dr. Rooney provides teachers with evidence-based techniques they can use with their most difficult-to-teach students."

—Daniel P. Hallahan
Charles S. Robb Professor of Education
Curry School of Education
University of Virginia
Charlottesville, VA

"Having used Dr. Rooney's learning strategies for many years in public and private instructional settings, I can affirm their high-yield effectiveness. Best of all, students enjoy this 'take charge' approach to their own learning. The strategies are logical, concise, and excellent for students to achieve improved understanding, retention, and memory retrieval for concepts. This book is a must for teachers who want to help their students become independent, self-confident, and successful learners!"

—Rebecca H. Aldred, MEd
Reading Consultant and Private Tutor
Ivy Creek School
Charlottesville, VA

"A gate barring success often needs but the right key. *Strategies for Learning* provides keys to unlock the knowledge of how to learn for those who always possessed the ability to learn. The knowledge, instinct, dedication, and passion of Karen Rooney gives a special clarity and power to her instructional recommendations. I wish my teachers had this book when I was in school."

—G. Emerson Dickman, JD
Immediate Past President
The International Dyslexia Association
Maywood, NJ

"A practical reference, this book adds useful learning strategies to teachers' toolboxes. All students, whether or not they have learning disabilities, benefit from practicing how to learn!"

—Patricia W. Newhall
Associate Director
Landmark School Outreach Program
Prides Crossing, MA

"This book contains easy-to-implement strategies to successfully develop and maximize learning for all students."

—Loukea Kovanis-Wilson
Chemistry Instructor
Clarkston High School
Clarkston, MI

"Dr. Rooney—You first put me on the road for success with the study skills you taught me. How they have paid off! Thank you."

Patrick Marshall Higgins
Lieutenant
United States Army USMA 08
Glen Allen, VA

Strategies

for

LEARNING

EMPOWERING STUDENTS FOR SUCCESS, GRADES 9–12

Karen J. Rooney

CORWIN
A SAGE Company

The study strategies in this book can also be done using software that is available through the Web site of Educational Enterprises, Inc., at www.krooney.com. Educational Enterprises, Inc., develops instructional materials and provides educational assessment, strategy instruction, consultation, professional development, and advocacy for children, adolescents, and adults. Please visit www.krooney.com to obtain additional information.

For information:

Corwin
A SAGE Company
2455 Teller Road
Thousand Oaks, California 91320
(800) 233-9936
Fax: (800) 417-2466
www.corwinpress.com

SAGE Ltd.
1 Oliver's Yard
55 City Road
London EC1Y 1SP
United Kingdom

SAGE India Pvt. Ltd.
B 1/I 1 Mohan Cooperative Industrial Area
Mathura Road, New Delhi 110 044
India

SAGE Asia-Pacific Pte. Ltd.
33 Pekin Street #02-01
Far East Square
Singapore 048763

Printed in the United States of America

Library of Congress Cataloging-in-Publication Data

Rooney, Karen J.
Strategies for learning : empowering students for success, grades 9–12 / Karen J. Rooney.
   p. cm.
Includes bibliographical references and index.
ISBN 978-1-4129-7285-7 (cloth)
ISBN 978-1-4129-7286-4 (pbk.)
   1. Learning disabled children—Education (Secondary) 2. Study skills—Study and teaching (Secondary) 3. Remedial teaching. I. Title.

LC4704.74.R66 2010
371.9—dc22   2009021591

This book is printed on acid-free paper.

09   10   11   12   13   10 9 8 7 6 5 4 3 2 1

Acquisitions Editor:	David Chao
Editorial Assistants:	Brynn Saito and Sarah Bartlett
Production Editor:	Jane Haenel
Copy Editor:	Mark Bast
Typesetter:	C&M Digitals (P) Ltd.
Proofreader:	Dennis W. Webb
Indexer:	Terri Corry
Cover and Graphic Designer:	Michael Dubowe

Contents

PART VI: ORGANIZATION, TIME MANAGEMENT, AND SOLVING PROBLEMS

Preface

As is true of many of my colleagues, I did not enter the field of special education through the "front door." My love of reading and writing led me to become an English major in college, with a second major in education. I wanted to be able to share my fascination with language (reading and writing) to inspire the students I would teach in my English classes. It wasn't long before I realized teaching English was not going to be as easy as providing popular background music while I taught Beowulf and Chaucer; unfortunately, to my surprise, I had students in my class who could not read. Thus, the "back door" to special education opened and I eagerly entered.

As a secondary English teacher, I wanted to help every student in my class to be successful; however, since I was only one person and I had large classes, the task was daunting. Hours spent writing corrections on tests, homework assignments, and papers did not produce the outcomes I hoped for, and did not seem to change the performance of students who were struggling. Those students who were doing well would continue to do so; I wanted to help the students who lacked the skills, strategies, and organization needed to succeed in school. I realized many of my students did not know how to develop solid study strategies on their own, even if motivated to do so, and the traditional study skills I knew were not working for them. I needed to find out how I could teach these students more efficient ways to master content material, work with their teachers more effectively, and perform better on tests. I began to develop strategies that would provide explicit structures, guides, and templates that were not dependent on the student's prior knowledge, organizational skills, or ability to "know" what to do.

These students needed strategies that did not rely heavily on their judgment, that provided "concrete" guides, and that were as "user-friendly" as possible. Students with learning disabilities and/or attention disorders had to have instruction that was more intense, explicit, and recursive than other students to "learn how to learn." Over the years, the strategies I developed while helping students to be more successful evolved into the program titled *Independent Strategies for Efficient Study*. To make sure the program was rigorous enough for students with learning disabilities and attention disorders, three studies were conducted, and the results demonstrated significant improvement in classroom grades when the strategies were implemented (Rooney, 1998). The strategies in this book are taken from that program, which has been taught to students with learning disabilities/attention disorders in clinical, private, and public settings since 1984.

At the secondary level, students need help at the skill level to improve reading, writing, spelling, and math, but they also need strategies that organize their learning to meet the demands of a variety of content areas/disciplines. The strategies in this book have been honed to create systems that are explicit, intense, and reiterative to improve performance, enable students to access the general education curriculum, and manage content across subject areas. The strategies may initially be implemented with assistance, but the goal is to develop independent use at some level as soon as possible. Even if adult assistance is needed initially, the strategies produce models that can transfer to independent use to increase self-esteem and confidence. Since the strategies teach students "how to learn," "how to organize," and "how to process information," lifelong learning is supported because the basic strategies remain the same even though the content may become more complex.

My hope is that the strategies in this book will help you empower your students, whether in the general education curriculum, in inclusive, co-taught or collaborative classes, in homeschooling situations, in private schools, or in special education settings. Additional resources at the ends of the chapters provide references for information and research related to the general principles underlying the strategies presented in this book.

ADDITIONAL RESOURCES

Rooney, K. (1998). *Independent strategies for efficient study*. Richmond, VA: Educational Enterprises. (Web site: www.krooney.com)

This is the original manual that was used as a reference tool for students and teachers after completing instruction in the *Independent Strategies for Efficient Study* program.

Swanson, L., Hoskyn, M., & Lee, C. (1999). *Interventions for students with learning disabilities: A meta-analysis of treatment outcomes*. New York: Guilford Press.

This book reviews the treatment outcomes for interventions with learning-disability students and also establishes the improvement in performance when strategy instruction is included in the intervention.

Acknowledgments

Corwin gratefully acknowledges the contributions of the following individuals:

Loukea Kovanis-Wilson
Chemistry Instructor
Clarkston High School
Clarkston, MI

Patricia W. Newhall
Associate Director
Landmark School Outreach Program
Prides Crossing, MA

Marilyn Steneken
Life Science Teacher
Sparta Middle School
Sparta, NJ

About the Author

 **Karen J. Rooney** is director of Educational Enterprises, Inc. in Richmond, Virginia. She earned her PhD in special education at the University of Virginia (major areas: special education, psychology, research) and holds licenses in English, Grades 7 through 12, in New York; and English, Grades 7 through 12, as well as learning disabilities, Grades K through 12, in Virginia. Karen has taught in both private and public sectors and was the educational specialist in a multidisciplinary clinic before becoming director of The Learning Resource Center and founder of The Attention Disorders Clinic. She is a past member of the national board of the International Dyslexia Association and is the 2007 recipient of the Rebecca Brock Richardson award.

Karen was selected to present a white paper on the importance of clinical judgment at the Learning Disabilities Summit in 2001, was a representative on the National Joint Committee on Learning Disabilities, served as the Children's Action Network representative for the Division for Learning Disabilities of the Council for Exceptional Children (CEC), and participated in the Expert Work Group to develop CEC's position regarding response to intervention. Currently, she is a past president of the Division for Learning Disabilities of the Council for Exceptional Children and serves on the Steering Committee of the National Adolescent Literacy Coalition.

Karen provides direct services to children, adolescents, and adults who need to improve their performance. She conducts assessments, provides educational consultation, and teaches the program titled *Independent Strategies for Efficient Study*. She also provides professional development on topics related to literacy skill development, learning disabilities, attention disorders, strategy training, and response-to-intervention. She has also published teaching materials such as *Wordstorming: A Tutorial Program for Parents, Teachers and Tutors*; *Reverse Diagramming*; and *Independent Strategies for Efficient Study: Upper Elementary/ Middle School Level* (www.krooney.com) and is currently developing a booklet to facilitate communication between parents and their young children.

Introduction 1

Knowing how to learn and study is an important part of the learning process and can make the difference between success and failure at the secondary level; unfortunately, many students, particularly students who have learning disabilities and attention disorders, enter high school without the study skills needed to be independent, efficient learners. These students need to be taught explicit strategies that will guide their thinking, facilitate comprehension, and support attention. These strategies should be simple, concrete, and efficient; should be taught using direct instruction (modeling, guided practice, independent practice); and should produce cumulative study systems to support retention, review, and test preparation.

Some students develop strategies that make them successful on their own, but other students, particularly those with learning disabilities and attention disorders, must be taught how to learn through direct, explicit instruction. Teaching clear, specific, evidence-based strategies is necessary to enable these students to access the general education curriculum. To expect one or two teachers, who may or may not have much special education background, to meet all the special needs of the students in the classroom setting is not realistic; teaching students strategies that empower them to be successful, independent learners and to build self-esteem should be the goal. For the secondary student, "learning how to learn" is critical to achieve, not only in school, but also in the workplace and postsecondary settings where less support will be available.

This book presents a collection of strategies that have been used to improve the performance of secondary students as well as individuals in workplace training programs. The research reported in the manual *Independent Strategies for Efficient Study* (Rooney, 1998) has demonstrated the efficacy of the strategies for students with attention problems, learning disabilities, and underachievement. The strategies are designed to activate the individual in the learning process through simple approaches that organize the process, incorporate isolation/reformatting/retrieval practice, and use explicit guides (such as format) to reduce the demands on the student's judgment or prior knowledge. After initial models, approaches, or techniques have been learned, the strategies need to be used and practiced, during instruction or through independent use, until organized learning is an automatic response to academic work.

BEFORE READING THIS BOOK

Since this book contains many strategies to meet the diverse needs of students, teachers, and subject areas, here are some suggestions for using the strategies. It is important to realize that the strategies

- do not have to be taught and implemented all at once, which could be overwhelming to some students;
- can be selected based on the individual needs of the student or the specific content area (possibly only one or two basic strategies at first) or can be selected to provide a curriculum for a learning-strategies class;
- may be used during instruction/homework assignments or be taught to individual students, even if the other students in the class do not need to use the strategies;
- can be used with as much or as little support as necessary based on the individual needs of the student;
- can be incorporated into instructional approaches or may be taught as separate study strategies;
- may need to be rewarded to support use if motivation is a concern (e.g., giving a grade or reward for using a strategy);
- need to be presented to students as changes in formats or approaches rather than extra work;
- should be explained in terms of increased efficacy, intensity, and ease of review to motivate use by the student;
- need to be taught using direct instruction that includes application of the strategy on a task so the student experiences success right away; and
- can be developed as study materials for use by the class (such as in peer-tutoring sessions or student study groups) or may be used by individual students.

The material in this book should be viewed as a collection of a wide range of evidence-based strategies that have improved the performance of struggling students, including those with learning disabilities/attention disorders, and can be selected, adapted, and implemented as needed based on the needs of the student or class, the style of the teacher, the instructional setting, the demands of the curriculum, and the motivation of the student.

BEFORE TEACHING THE STRATEGIES

It is very important to develop an understanding of the general principles, techniques, and important concepts underlying the development of the strategies in this book. As you are learning the strategies, please keep the following thoughts in mind so that you can see how the strategies are structured to guide thinking, be "user-friendly," and support learning as well as to be implemented in ways that match your particular preferences, needs, or subject area/setting:

- Students can use index cards, paper, or computer software (see **www.krooney.com**) to produce the review systems that support learning, studying, and test taking.

- The strategies can be used during the initial instruction or as homework assignments, with entire classes or with individual students; some teachers develop a "class set" that students can use to review and prepare for tests rather than have individual sets of cards or notes.

- Selected strategies may be chosen to develop a basic learning-strategies course, may be selected for specific content areas, or may be tailored to an individual student's needs by selecting appropriate strategies from the program.

- The strategy training can be built into instruction, note taking, and homework assignments, but it is designed to present models that students can eventually use as independently as possible when they have to learn information in school or, eventually, in the workplace.

- Motivation is an important component of learning for the secondary student and should be considered when planning strategy training. The more motivated the student is, the more the strategies can be taught as a way to improve academic performance by teaching the student specific strategies. The less motivated the student is, the more the use of the strategies will need to be part of the instruction, in classroom activities, or assigned for homework, which will result in credit for the use of the strategy.

- Even when the strategies are implemented in the context of instruction, rather than independence, the models are so explicit that the process can generalize to new situations when the student may be more motivated (such as passing the driver's license test or maintaining eligibility for sports).

- The strategies have been taught to students on an individual basis or in small-group settings. Six hours of instruction are required to teach the basic strategies, but strategies can be selected by the teacher based on the student's needs, which would require less time. For example, the textbook note-taking strategy and reduced note-taking strategy for classroom instruction may be all one student needs to learn; another student may just need the writing strategies.

GENERAL PRINCIPLES, TECHNIQUES, AND IMPORTANT CONCEPTS

And now, it is important to become familiar with the terminology used in this book:

- **Advance organizers** are forms or graphics that establish the task or organizational demands in advance of the processing to support thinking right from the start of the task and produce "reminders" to finish parts of the task that have not been completed.

- **Cards and column formats** refer to systems using flash cards (e.g., index cards) or paper folded in half lengthwise to create two columns. Some teachers refer to the latter as a "hot dog" fold. The formats provide a structure to produce review systems that use isolation, reformatting, and retrieval practice. Students can choose any one of the formats (rectangles, squares, grids, charts, cards, or two columns) based on preference. Computerized versions are also available at **www.krooney.com.**

- **Concrete guides** refer to guides, starting points, or hints that are very explicit and do not depend on judgment, prior knowledge, or reasoning. For example, looking for subtitles by looking for a different style of font is a concrete guide. Looking for a capital letter to identify a name is another concrete guide.

- **Cover sheets** refer to the use of blank paper or cards to cover or block all information except the information that should be the target of attention. Visual distraction is reduced and focus of attention is supported.

- **Isolation** refers to the removal of information from text or other material so the focus of attention is artificially targeted on the appropriate information. Surrounding the information with white space forces attention to the information and guides memory processing since no other information is available during processing.

- **Manipulatives** refer to specific techniques that involve motor activity, such as making notations or card sorting to help sustain attention, increase intensity, and support processing.

- **Multisensory processing** refers to an approach that integrates visual, auditory, and tactile processing through seeing the material (visual), using self-talk (auditory), and writing or sorting (tactile).

- **Reformatting/rephrasing** means changing the information to a new format or having the student explain the information verbally or in writing. The goal is to reduce rote memorization and "busy work" that does not engage the student's thinking. Information should always be reformatted (such as changing standard textbook paragraphs into lists or literature text into charts) or put into the student's own words.

- **Retrieval practice** requires the student to recall information from memory without support. The use of index cards or two-column formats produce retrieval practice systems, since the names, numbers, terms, and topics are isolated on the front of the card or first column, and the related information is hidden from view on the back of the card or second column.

- **Review systems** refer to the production of some type of summary of the critical information at the time of the initial processing to support retention.

- **Squares, grids, or charts** refer to visual organizers that are more categorical and are used to organize information to focus attention, to highlight details and main ideas, and to clearly identify concepts. Rectangles, squares, charts, or grids are made by folding a sheet of paper in half lengthwise and then folding again to produce four squares. The sections are labeled by category, and notes are taken within each section as appropriate. If more than four sections are needed, a second page is made so that the categories can all be seen while the work is being done. The only time information is placed on the back of the sheet is when the room in any of the sections is not large enough.

- **Visual anchors** refer to supports for memory problems, such as short-term memory or working memory (the ability to manipulate information in memory without visual support) deficits. The visual anchors are simply information that is written down immediately to "anchor" the information and bypass memory during subsequent processing.

- **Wheels** refer to ovals that support processing by separating information into details and main ideas in a visual display. The wheel is simply an oval with the main idea or concept within the wheel (oval) and the details or related information spiked around the outside of the wheel. Wheels differ from mindmapping, webbing, spidering, or clustering because the format will always be linear (one wheel placed underneath the previous wheel) and will never branch out sideways. The linear format will organize the sequence visually to display the order of the task demands or establish a logical progression of ideas rather than produce a more scattered array of ideas.

The terminology should be used during instruction and when describing the strategies to other teachers and parents so that the concepts underlying the strategies will be understood.

ADDITIONAL RESOURCES

Rooney, K. (1998). *Independent strategies for efficient study*. Richmond, VA: Educational Enterprises.
Rooney, K. Web site: www.krooney.com.

Part I

Vocabulary and Note Taking When Reading

2 Vocabulary

Vocabulary development is essential to strong academic performance. Knowing the meanings, multiple meanings, and nuances of words supports reading, writing, and listening; having a weak vocabulary can interfere with comprehension across all subject areas, even math. Some students have difficulty with receptive language, which means they have trouble learning, understanding, and retaining word knowledge or retrieving words quickly from memory, which interferes with fluency. Often, these students have nonverbal strengths such as art talent, creativity (building elaborate Lego constructions, demonstrating musical talent, acting, making jewelry), or strong visualization skills, which can be incorporated into the learning process when learning verbal information. The strategy called *pictorials* is one way of achieving this goal.

Pictorials are visual representations of verbal concepts through the use of pictures or diagrams. The approach is very simple, but it can be used for English vocabulary to develop visual images and conceptual representations to support processing. The student draws a picture that forces comprehension of the concept, creates an association that will facilitate retention, and produces a review system to increase speed of retrieval (word retrieval). It is very important that the student should make the picture based on his or her own personal experience and should include all the details related to the concept.

When I first began to recognize that many of my students were very visually oriented, I spent hours finding pictures in magazines and newspapers to match the vocabulary words or concepts I was teaching. One day I stopped that practice immediately when, in a tone of exasperation, one of my young students shared that she thought it was hard enough to learn the vocabulary words without having to memorize pictures too! Suddenly, I realized she could draw a picture that made sense to her, involved her thinking, and connected with her prior knowledge. No more magazine hunts for me!

If the picture, context, or example is supplied by someone else, it is only another piece of information to be learned. The association must be natural so that it will connect with known information, be embedded in a familiar context, and be easier to retrieve.

LEARNING VOCABULARY

Either index cards or paper with a column format is recommended to develop review systems that facilitate frequent repetition to support retention and develop faster retrieval.

If using the cards, the front should isolate the word from the definition, which is placed on the back of the card. If using a two-column format, the first column is like the front of the index card and the second column is used the same way as the back of the card. The student

- writes the vocabulary word (isolation) on the front of a card (or the first column of a two-column format);
- writes the meaning on the back of the card (or in second column) by listing important parts of the definition rather than copying words in a rote manner; and
- makes up an example, rephrased definition, or drawing/diagram under the definition on the back of the card. The concept, context, or visual will facilitate processing, attention, and retention, and the cards will produce a cumulative-review system to practice retrieval.

The cards should be reviewed frequently, and retention can be supported by having the students write a story that includes all the newly learned words to embed the new vocabulary in a meaningful context.

Student Sample: Example

Plesiosaurus

Figure 2.1   Vocabulary Card: Example

Prehistoric dinosaur
Loch Ness Monster

Figure 2.2   Vocabulary Card: Example

Student Sample: Rephrasing

Photosynthesis

Figure 2.3   Vocabulary Card: Rephrasing

1. Process by which green plants and other organisms turn carbon dioxide and water into carbohydrates and oxygen,
2. using light energy trapped by chlorophyll

The way green plants that have chlorophyll make CO_2 and H_2O into carbs and oxygen using light energy

Figure 2.4   Vocabulary Card: Rephrasing

Student Sample: Pictorial

The Federal Reserve Act divided the United States into districts and placed a Federal Reserve Bank within each district to provide support for banks within the district.

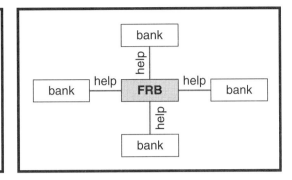

Figure 2.5   Vocabulary Card: Pictorial

Figure 2.6   Vocabulary Card: Pictorial

Student Example Using Two-Column Format Rather Than Cards

(Example) Plesiosaurus	Prehistoric dinosaur Loch Ness Monster
(Rephrasing) Photosynthesis	1. Process by which green plants and other organisms turn carbon dioxide and water into carbohydrates and oxygen, 2. using light energy trapped by chlorophyll. The way green plants that have chlorophyll turn CO_2 and H_2O into carbs and oxygen using light energy.
(Pictorial) Federal Reserve Act	Divided the United States into districts and placed a Federal Reserve Bank within each district to provide support for banks within the district.

Figure 2.7   Vocabulary Two-Column Format

ADDITIONAL RESOURCES

Scruggs, T. E., & Mastropieri, M. A. (2007). Science learning in special education: The case for constructed versus instructed learning. *Exceptionality, 15,* 57–74.

This article discusses learning in a specific content area (science) and was written by researchers who have developed and researched mnemonic strategies that have been shown to improve comprehension and retention.

Wolgemuth, J. R., Cobb, R. B., & Alwell, M. (2008). The effects of mnemonic interventions on academic outcomes for youth with disabilities. *Learning Disabilities Research & Practice, 23,* 1–10.

In this study, the positive effects of mnemonic strategies were validated, and the data show the importance of such support at the secondary level.

3 Note Taking When Reading Material With Subtitles (Textbooks, Handouts, and Web Site Material)

As an English teacher and a specialist in the area of learning disabilities, one of the most challenging tasks was helping students master content material (such as science, history, or social studies) when they seemed unable to distinguish between important and unimportant information. As a student, Jim, shared, "I just never knew what I was supposed to learn so I'd have to learn everything; I didn't read the book and figured I'd wait and hope my teacher taught what I should know." With this approach, he did not have the prior knowledge, conceptual understanding, or advance organization that the students who read the text had, which made him less able to obtain what he needed from the classroom instruction.

When reading textbooks, successful students focus on the details and topics that are important. Traditional strategies that rely on the student's judgment may not provide sufficient support for students with learning disabilities and attention disorders. For example, advising students to highlight the important details is inefficient because the strategy works only for the students who know what those details are; if a student doesn't know or can't distinguish the important from the unimportant, the learning process is compromised, even if the student tries to use the strategy.

With my struggling students, I used small-group instruction to try to help them recognize the important details and topics. I spent hours working with books that had exercises related to identifying details and main ideas. We read selections of text; they answered questions related to the details and main ideas, and then we discussed why the correct answers were right. Over time, I began to realize that there was little transfer from the instruction; students continued to have trouble identifying the important details and topics on their own. It became clear to me that the students had to use the format of the book to provide structure, guide their thinking, and target the important information.

The use of note-taking strategies during reading results in a systematic approach that enables students to learn more effectively and teachers to work more efficiently with their students. Teachers can review the cards or columns to make sure the study systems are complete and accurate; often, weaker students have study materials that are inaccurate or incomplete—which hinders test taking even if the student studies for the test.

Students can easily use the cards or columns to work with their content teachers by having the cards reviewed to make sure they are complete and accurate. If the student can't find the information to put on the back of the card or in the second column, the student can take the cards or columns with the unknown name, number, term, or topic identified to a teacher for assistance. Instead of the teacher having to spend a great deal of time trying to identify what help a struggling student needs or the student's not seeking help because he or she does not know the questions to ask, the strategy produces a review system that facilitates communication between students and their teachers.

The cards or columns should be completed at the time of the initial reading so the time prior to a test is used to review, not make, the cards or columns. The system is cumulative to support test preparation. If the test is on Chapters 10 through 15, the cards or columns from those chapters are reviewed. For exam review, the student will have a card or entry in a column that tracks all the names, numbers, terms, and topics from the semester or year in a review system that supports focus of attention (isolation), comprehension (reformatting or rephrasing), and retrieval practice (pulling up information that is not visible).

The systems actually provide "practice tests" prior to the test or exam to identify areas needing additional study, make sure the information can be retrieved when needed, and speed recall when taking tests or exams. The review will track retention over time and allow students who need more review to study the cards or columns as frequently as needed to support retention.

CARD FORMAT

This system should be used when doing any assigned reading in a textbook, handout, or Web site. If grades are low in a class, the system should be used on the textbook chapters that match the topics being presented in class, even if the chapters are not assigned. The strategy will build prior knowledge, and the classroom presentation will then deepen the student's understanding of the material.

The strategy approaches the assigned reading as units of text divided by subtitles. The student is told that the subtitles will be a different size, color, or font and can be identified by just looking at the text. For example, the following is a subtitle followed by text material:

Influence of Twain

Mark Twain is widely regarded as one of the greatest American authors, and he is also considered to be one of the greatest influences on the development of the American character as we know it.

As soon as the student can identify a subtitle, the student is ready to learn the strategy.

During the initial instruction, students are told explicitly what they will be identifying when taking notes. Have the student draw a square or use a card to make two sections; one is labeled *Details* and the other is labeled *Main Ideas*.

In the Details section, the student should write the following:

- Names (capital letter is the clue)
- Numbers (related to time)
- Terms (words I need to know)

In the Main Ideas section, the student should write the following:

- Subtitles
- Information at the beginning of a section or chapter (preview)
- Information at the end of a section or chapter (review or check)
- Information in margins

The purpose of this instruction is to clearly identify an explicit guide the student can use while learning the strategy.

Basic Strategy Using Cards

Tell the student to read any material that is found between the main title and the first subtitle, which is the introduction, to develop a framework to support comprehension.

At the first subtitle, the student should do the following:

1. Read the subtitle and the section under the subtitle. While reading, names (such as people and places) and numbers related to time and terms (words students don't know—not just bold-print words) are written on separate index cards. One, two, or three words will be the most that will be written on a card. Only the word/words or number by itself should be on a card. For example, if the words *Missouri*, *1853*, and *Calaveras County* were in a passage, each would appear on a separate card.

2. Return to the subtitle and turn it into the best test question, making the question as hard as possible or similar to actual test questions that have been used on past tests by his or her teachers. The question is written on one side of an index card, and the answer to the question is reformatted from the paragraphs into bullet lists on the back of the same card, producing a main-idea question and answer card to put in the study system.

3. Repeat Steps 1 and 2 on all the sections to be covered so that a set of cards comprising details and main ideas is produced.

4. Review the cards by recalling the information that is not visible from memory, going from front to back and then back to front. Going both ways with the cards practices retrieval of the names, numbers, terms, and topics as well as the related information. This will serve as a practice test to identify areas needing additional study and increase speed of retrieval.

If an answer is unknown, the card is placed in one pile. If an answer is known, the card is placed in a separate pile, resulting in two piles, one called *not sure* and the other called *sure*. The *sure* pile is set aside, and the student continues to work with the *not sure* pile. For the details in the *not sure* pile, the student goes back into the text to find the answer or asks someone else what the answer is; the answer is then written on the back of the card to intensify the processing of the information that did not transfer into long-term memory. The detail cards as well as any *not sure* main idea cards are reviewed until all cards are in the *sure* pile. All cards should be made up during the reading, not just prior to a quiz or test, to support reading comprehension, and only the main idea cards will have information listed on the back of the card during the reading. Detail cards will have writing on the back only if the student could not recall the information; the purpose of this is to reduce some of the writing and minimize time spent taking notes during the reading.

If written production is a concern, the use of a computer or dictation, rather than writing, can be used as an accommodation; however, the student must do the thinking. If dictation is used, the student should stop the device (tape player, Dictaphone, or computer) after hearing the name, number, term, or topic to allow for time to retrieve the information from memory.

Student Sample

Mark Twain

Twain's Youth

Mark Twain (a pen name for Samuel Langhorne Clemens) was born in 1835 in Missouri and spent much of his youth along the Mississippi River. He began a widely varied professional life at age 12 as a printer for his brother's newspaper. This occupation led him to many American cities, such as New York, Philadelphia, and New Orleans.

Twain's Riverboat Days

In 1853, Twain began work as a steamship pilot and continued to do so until the Civil War. This occupation had a powerful influence on Twain and is vividly depicted in many of his greatest writings. Twain's riverboat career was cut short, however, when the Civil War caused the closing of the Mississippi River.

Mark Twain's Literary Years

When the river was closed due to the war, Twain tried his hand at mining in Nevada and soon became a newspaper editor. After Nevada, he moved to San Francisco and became a reporter. While living in San Francisco, he had his first literary success with "The Celebrated Jumping Frog of Calaveras County." In 1870, Twain was married and he moved to Connecticut, where he devoted his energy to writing. It was during this phase of his life that he published many of

(Continued)

(Continued)

his most cherished works, such as *The Prince and the Pauper*, *The Adventures of Huckleberry Finn*, and *The Adventures of Tom Sawyer*.

Twain's Last Years

Although Twain was very successful in his writing career, unfortunate investments led to his financial ruin and he was forced to declare bankruptcy. Twain conducted a lecture tour to improve his financial position; however, the last 10 years of his life were filled with loss, including the deaths of two daughters and his wife. In 1910, Twain passed away.

The following cards were made for the previous text:

First Section

Mark Twain	Samuel Langhorne Clemens
1835	Missouri
Mississippi River	12 years old
New York	Philadelphia
New Orleans	(front of card) Give a description of Twain's youth

(back of card)
1. born in Missouri
2. grew up along Mississippi River
3. a printer
4. lived in New York, Philadelphia, and New Orleans

Second Section

1853	(front of card) Describe Twain's riverboat days.
Civil War	(back of card) 1. steamship pilot 2. 1853–Civil War 3. powerful influence

Third Section

Nevada	San Francisco
"The Celebrated Jumping Frog of Calaveras County"	1870
Connecticut	*The Prince and the Pauper*
The Adventures of Huckleberry Finn	*The Adventures of Tom Sawyer*
(front of card) Describe Twain's literary years	(back of card) 1. mining 2. newspaper editor 3. 1870: married 4. Connecticut: wrote his most famous books

Fourth Section

Last 10 years	(front of card) Describe Twain's last years.

1910	(back of card)
	  1. bankruptcy
	  2. lecture tour
	  3. loss of wife and daughters
	  4. Twain dies in 1910

PAPER/COLUMN FORMAT

If either the teacher or student prefers to use paper rather than cards, an alternative is to use the column organizer. Make two columns by folding a sheet of paper in half lengthwise (or draw a line down the center). The first column operates just like the front of an index card, and the second column acts like the back of the index card.

While reading, the student should do the following:

1. Write names (such as people and places) and numbers related to time and terms (words students don't know—not just bold-print words) in the first column. Only the word/words or number by itself should be recorded. For example, if the words *Missouri, 1853,* and *Calaveras County* were in a passage, each would appear separately with some "white space" (usually two or three skipped lines) in between each item.

2. Return to the subtitle and turn it into the best test question, making the question as hard as possible or as similar as possible to actual test questions that have been used on past tests by his or her teachers. The question is written in the first column, and the answer to the question is reformatted from the paragraphs to a list in the second column, producing a main-idea question and answer.

3. Repeats Steps 1 and 2 on all the sections to be covered.

When studying using the columns, the paper is folded so the first column is in view; the related information in the hidden second column is recalled from memory. The columns are then folded the other way so the hidden names, numbers, terms, and topics are recalled while looking at the listed information. If the information related to name, number, or term can't be recalled, the information should be obtained from the reading and written in the corresponding second column; if the information related to the topic can't be recalled, the list in the second column should be reviewed.

Student Sample

Names, Numbers, Terms, Topics	Related Information
Mark Twain	
Samuel Langhorne Clemens	
1835	
Missouri	
Mississippi River	
12 years old	
New York	
Philadelphia	
New Orleans	
Give a description of Twain's youth.	1. Born in Missouri 2. Grew up along Mississippi River 3. A printer 4. Lived in New York, Philadelphia, and New Orleans
1853	
Civil War	
Describe Twain's riverboat days.	1. Steamship pilot 2. 1853–Civil War
Nevada	

(Continued)

(Continued)

Names, Numbers, Terms, Topics	Related Information
San Francisco	
1870	
"The Celebrated Jumping Frog of Calaveras County"	
Connecticut	
The Prince and the Pauper	
The Adventures of Huckleberry Finn	
The Adventures of Tom Sawyer	
Describe Twain's literary years.	1. Mining 2. Newspaper editor 3. 1870: married 4. Connecticut: wrote most famous books
Last 10 years	
1910	
Describe Twain's last years.	1. Bankruptcy 2. Lecture tour 3. Loss of wife and daughters 4. Twain dies in 1910

ADDITIONAL RESOURCES

Bulgren, J., Deshler, D. D., & Lenz, B. K. (2007). Engaging adolescents with LD in higher order thinking about history concepts using integrated content enhancement routines. *Journal of Learning Disabilities, 40*(2), 121–133.

This article recognizes the demands for acquisition and use of content knowledge and uses content enhancement routines to demonstrate planning, teaching, and evaluating higher order thinking skills.

Strickland, D. S., & Alvermann, D. E. (2004). *Bridging the literacy gap grades 4–12.* New York: Teachers College Press.

This book identifies the challenges at the secondary level, provides information about the needs of diverse learners, and discusses "closing the gap" as a schoolwide concern.

Note Taking 4
Using Shortcut
Advance
Organizers

Some students need as much structure as possible but want to do the minimum amount of work. As one student said, "I know the strategy using subtitles works, but I'm not going to do that much work, even if I would get a good grade." For those students, note taking has to be very structured and must be very efficient.

The shortcut advance organizer strategy is recommended for most students to use, but it should be taught after instruction in the general strategy to help students understand the process underlying the use of the text format.

Nonfiction reading material is typically organized to provide guidance in identifying the important details and main ideas, but often students do not utilize the organization to their advantage. If the textbook, handout, or Web site material has identification items or questions identified at the beginning or end of the section or chapter, or in the margins, the note-taking process can be very explicit. By making cards or columns that identify the important details and main ideas prior to reading the text, the student creates an overview of the material—which supports comprehension—as well as a system that will intensify processing/focus of attention and require retrieval of learned information from memory to prepare for tests.

Often, students are required to read text and answer questions at the end of the section to support processing and retention. Though this process may work for some students, many students will find answering the questions and taking tests on the material they read to be problematic. These students may feel as though they have completed the assigned reading and will be well prepared to take a test; however, if students do not practice retrieval of the information from memory, test taking may be affected by problems with recall, even though the material was "learned." It is important for students to not only use note taking to support reading comprehension, but also to use the notes as "practice tests" before taking the real tests to identify areas needing additional study, reduce careless errors, and increase automaticity of recall.

SHORTCUT ADVANCE ORGANIZER: USING CARDS

Before beginning to read, the student should do the following:

- Look at the beginning of the chapter to see if names (people you will meet), numbers (dates you need to know), terms or vocabulary, and topics or main ideas are identified in a preview section. If such help is available, the student writes each name, number, and term on separate index cards with no other information on the card; each topic (not statements or questions, but the topic of any statement or question) should also be placed on separate index cards.

If the topic is presented as a question, the question should not be copied verbatim, but should be reformatted to engage thinking and relate the information to the topic, reducing memorization of questions and answers. Again, just the topics should be identified and written on the cards. The resulting cards will produce an advance organizer that supports focus, comprehension, and note taking. Making the cards identifies the important information in advance, provides an overview, and guides note taking, which reduces processing demands during the reading.

Next, the student needs to do the following:

- Check the end of the section, chapter, or margins to see if any additional names, numbers, terms, or topics are provided as a review or comprehension check in order to add them to the set of cards. Questions under the heading of "critical thinking" often provide additional topics that should be added.
- Place the cards within sight when reading the text. When any name, number, term, or topic that is written on a card is encountered in the text, the student reformats the related information from the text (which is likely in a paragraph) into a list.

Making the list intensifies the focus of attention on the critical pieces of information. The cards then produce a cumulative review system, with the name, number, term, or topic isolated on one side of the card and the related information listed on the back of each card.

The cards should be reviewed front to back and back to front, until all the details and the related information can be easily recalled from memory.

For some students, secondary textbooks are so laden with information that the use of this explicit strategy to guide note taking enables them to handle complex text that would be overwhelming without having such a literal guide.

Student Sample

Chapter 10: The Nixon Years (Chapter Preview)

People	Dates	Topics
E. Howard Hunt G. Gordon Liddy John Dean H. R. Haldeman Gerald Ford	1974	Two break-ins White House Horrors The Plumbers Nixon's resignation White House tapes

The Nixon years were turbulent and revealed activities that were shocking to the American people. Day after day, the headlines carried disturbing facts, confessions, and reports of illegal activities that involved the highest officials in the land.

Break-Ins

On August 9, 1974, Richard Nixon resigned from the presidency in the wake of the most serious constitutional crisis in modern U.S. politics. The culmination of a series of crimes described by John Mitchell, Nixon's attorney general and closest adviser, as the "White House Horrors" led to Richard Nixon's resignation. Since impeachment proceedings were underway, his resignation seemed to many an escape from further investigation and remains one of the most important and enigmatic chapters in U.S. history. The break-in at the Democratic National Committee (DNC) Headquarters on June 17, 1972, was actually the second break-in perpetrated by the White House. There were illegally installed room microphones and phone bugs as well as photography of files and documents. Neither the objective of the documents search during the break-ins nor the desired outcome of these activities was ever fully established, nor did Senate investigators receive answers to their questions.

Burglars

The first break-in at the DNC headquarters was on May 28, 1972. President Nixon was in Moscow on the first summit to be held there by the Soviet Union and United States. The crisis began with the June 17, 1972, arrest of five men in the DNC Headquarters at the Watergate office complex. The next day, two of President Nixon's main operators, who were former intelligence officials, were arrested after overseeing the sabotage operation with electronic equipment in a nearby Howard Johnson's motel. The two men, E. Howard Hunt (White House aide and retired Central Intelligence Agency agent) and G. Gordon Liddy (counsel for the Committee to Re-Elect the President, and an ex-FBI agent), worked for the president of the United States in the White House. Hunt's early CIA covert activities had occurred during the overthrow of the Guatemalan government, and he later was the "mastermind" of the Bay of Pigs invasion in Cuba. Hunt's CIA background provided him with his team of burglars. They were all linked to the CIA: ex-CIA agent James McCord, three former CIA operatives Hunt commanded during the Bay of Pigs incident, Frank Sturgis, Rolando Martinez, and Virilio Gonzalez, as well as Bernard Barker, Hunt's liaison in Miami during the Bay of Pigs. Howard Hunt worked for Charles Colson in the White House, and Charles Colson worked under John Ehrlichman and, later, John Dean.

Inside the White House

John Dean was hired as counsel to the White House in November 1972, and he set to work on a number of illegal operations involving the Internal Revenue Service and the famous "enemies" list. The young counsel was eager to serve the president and was one of the leaders of the Watergate scandal. Dean gave the famous "cancer on the presidency" testimony before the Senate Watergate Committee, which led to the crumbling of the conspiracy he helped create.

The Plumbers

H. R. Haldeman and John Ehrlichman were the direct connections to Nixon. These two men carried out orders from Nixon to blackmail senators and any others on the "enemies" list by initiating a White House political subversion campaign named The Plumbers. The name really fit since the first job was to "plug news leaks" in the government. They directed the cover-up from the oval office. Both were forced to resign in Nixon's attempt to "clean up" the situation.

Conclusion

President Nixon had "bugged" all White House business and offices. The tapes this system produced would lead directly to the president's resignation. He left the White House in order to keep his legal hold on the tapes, which, other than 200 hours of Nixon-edited tapes, had been mostly suppressed until roughly 3,000 of the estimated 6,000 were released in 1996. He would have had to hand them over to the courts and face impeachment if he did not resign, and the pardon he received from President Gerald Ford ensured that the crime would not be investigated further.

Section Review

Identification Items

1974, White House Horrors, E. Howard Hunt, G. Gordon Liddy, John Dean, H. R. Haldeman, The Plumbers, White House tapes, and Gerald Ford

Discussion Questions

1. Describe the two break-ins that occurred in 1972 and 1974.
2. Explain John Dean's role in the White House conspiracy.
3. Explain the purpose of The Plumbers, and state who was involved.
4. Why did President Nixon resign?

(Remember, cards are made before the student begins to read the text.)

Student Sample: Cards Using the Preview and Review Sections

E. Howard Hunt	G. Gordon Liddy
John Dean	H. R. Haldeman
Gerald Ford	1974

Two break-ins	White House Horrors
The Plumbers	Nixon's resignation

White House tapes

Student Sample: Cards Using the Section Review Only (When No Preview Section Is Available)

1974	White House Horrors
E. Howard Hunt	G. Gordon Liddy
John Dean	H. R. Haldeman
The Plumbers	White House tapes
Gerald Ford	Two break-ins

Role of John Dean	The Plumbers: Purpose and who was involved

Nixon's resignation

If only the Section Review is used, the details and topics will often be encountered in consecutive order (details in order and topics in order), which provides further support.

SHORTCUT ADVANCE ORGANIZER: USING PAPER/COLUMNS

If a teacher or student prefers to use paper, an alternative strategy is to use the column organizer. The student should follow these guidelines:

- Make two columns by folding a sheet of paper in half lengthwise (or draw a line down the center). The first column operates just like the front of an index card, and the second column acts like the back of an index card.
- Prior to reading, the names, numbers, terms, and topics from the preview section or review sections or margins are listed in the first column. Between names, numbers, and terms, approximately three or four lines on the paper are left blank; for topics, eight or nine lines are left blank.
- During the reading, related information is listed in the second column.

There is one disadvantage to using the paper format; the student has to estimate the amount of space, which is why explicit guidelines such as three to four lines for details and eight to nine lines for main ideas or topics are taught.

When studying using the columns, the paper is folded so the first column is in view; the related information in the hidden second column is recalled from memory. The columns are then folded the other way so the hidden names, numbers, terms, and topics are recalled while looking at the listed information.

Student Sample: Shortcut Setup Using the Preview and Review Sections

Names, Numbers, Terms, Topics	Related Information
E. Howard Hunt	
G. Gordon Liddy	

Names, Numbers, Terms, Topics	Related Information
John Dean	
H. R. Haldeman	
Gerald Ford	
1974	
Two break-ins	
White House Horrors	
The Plumbers	
Nixon's resignation	
White House Tapes	

Student Sample: Shortcut Setup Using the Section Review (When a Preview Section Is Not Available)

Names, Numbers, Terms, Topics	Related Information
1974	
White House Horrors	
E. Howard Hunt	
G. Gordon Liddy	

Names, Numbers, Terms, Topics	Related Information
John Dean	
H. R. Haldeman	
The Plumbers	
White House tapes	
Gerald Ford	
Two break-ins	
Role of John Dean	
The Plumbers: purpose and who was involved	
Nixon's resignation	

ADDITIONAL RESOURCES

Denton, C., & Vaughn, S. (2008). Adolescents with reading disabilities [Special issue]. *Learning Disabilities Research & Practice, 23*(2).

This special issue has articles that discuss reading and writing interventions with older children, identifying what we know and what we need to know about reading comprehension for adolescents with LD. It also addresses vocabulary instruction for older students.

Deshler, D. D., Robinson, S., & Mellard, D. F. (2004). Instructional principles for optimizing outcomes for adolescents with learning disabilities. In M. K. Riley & T. A. Citro (Eds.), *Best practices for inclusionary classroom: Leading researchers talk directly with teachers* (pp. 65–79). Weston, MA: Learning Disabilities Association Worldwide.

This chapter emphasizes the principles that should be in place to support performance-improving learning strategies. The principles presented in this article are based on a long history of experience and research and should be considered when designing and implementing interventions that will have the best outcomes for students.

Note Taking for Material Without Subtitles (Teacher Handouts, Review Sheets, or Class Notes) 5

At times, students are required to take notes when reading material without subtitles to provide any structured guidance, but students will still need to use strategies that provide a system to support comprehension and retention by producing cumulative review systems. After instruction in the basic strategy and the shortcut, students can rely on identifying names, numbers, terms, and topics, even if the format is not as explicit as when subtitles or preview and review formats are provided.

CARD FORMAT

Written notes or handouts should be tracked for details and main idea questions by using index cards to produce a flash card system for easy review. The cards should be reviewed frequently to prepare for taking a test on the material, and the cards should be saved to produce a cumulative system to review for an exam.

As the material is read, the student should do the following:

- Make study cards by writing all names, numbers, or terms and possible essay test questions on the front of index cards. The resulting set of cards will be a collection of details and main idea questions. As in the other strategies, names (such as people and places), numbers, and terms should be used as a guide for the identification of the details.
- Study the cards by asking how the detail is related to the material or by answering the test question.

- Divide the cards into a pile that is known for *sure* and one for which the student is *not sure* and continue working with the *not sure* cards by returning to the material to find the answers.
- Write the answers to the unsure cards on the backs of the index cards to increase the intensity for information that did not remain in memory.
- Review the cards until all the cards are known.

Cards will be cumulative so that the information from all the notes and handouts can be reviewed easily over time, using a practice test format.

Student Sample: Cards

The Renaissance was famous for literature written in the vernacular for the first time. This was of major importance because books were made available to the ordinary person. Most Renaissance literature dealt with humanism or religious subjects. The most famous writers were these men:

1. Dante: wrote *The Divine Comedy*

2. Francesco Petrarch: wrote classical literature and developed the sonnet

3. Niccolo Machiavelli: wrote *The Prince*, which said that a ruler did not need the approval of the people to rule

4. Thomas More: wrote *Utopia*, which outlined the perfect Christian society

Possibly the most famous man during the Renaissance was Leonardo da Vinci (1452–1519), who is known as the Universal Man. He was given this title because his work spanned so many areas. Da Vinci, who is known as a painter, engineer, anatomist, botanist, optician, and inventor, was brilliant. Perhaps he is best known as an artist. His most famous paintings are *The Last Supper* and the *Mona Lisa*. The Renaissance was very important in changing art, and this change is visible in da Vinci's work. Previously, most art dealt with religious content, but the new art was characterized by color, perspective, and shadow, which made the figures more lifelike. Da Vinci's works celebrated the human body.

Renaissance	Vernacular
Humanism	Dante
The Divine Comedy	Francesco Petrarch

Niccolo Machiavelli	*The Prince*
Thomas More	*Utopia*
Leonardo da Vinci	1452–1519
Why was da Vinci called the Universal Man?	*The Last Supper*
Mona Lisa	How did the Renaissance change art?

PAPER/COLUMN FORMAT

If paper is used as the material is read, the student should do the following:

- Write names, numbers, or terms and possible essay test questions in the first column, which will result in a cumulative system of details and main idea questions. As in the other strategies, names (such as people and places), numbers, and terms should be used as a guide for the identification of the details.
- Study by asking how the detail is related to the material or by answering the test question.

If the answer is known, no other action is needed. If the answer is unknown, the student finds the answer and writes the information in the second column.

Student Sample Using Two-Column Format

Names, Numbers, Terms, Topics	Related Information
Renaissance	
Vernacular	
Humanism	
Dante	
The Divine Comedy	
Francesco Petrarch	
Niccolo Machiavelli	
The Prince	
Thomas More	
Utopia	
Leonardo da Vinci	
1452–1519	

Names, Numbers, Terms, Topics	Related Information
Why was da Vinci called the Universal Man?	
The Last Supper	
Mona Lisa	
How did the Renaissance change art?	

ADDITIONAL RESOURCES

Klingner, J. K., Vaughn, S., & Boardman, A. (2007). *Teaching reading comprehension to students with learning difficulties.* New York: Guilford Press.

This book includes chapters on assessing reading comprehension, the role of vocabulary in reading comprehension, text structure, instructional practices, and strategy training.

Mastropieri, M. A., Berkeley, S., Scruggs, T. E., & Marshak, L. (2008). Improving content area instruction using evidenced based practices. *Insights on Learning Disabilities, 5*(1), 73–88.

This article discusses the use of explicit instruction, cognitive strategies, and self-regulation to improve the performance of students with diverse needs.

Torgeson, J. K., Houston, D. D., Rissman, L. M., Decker, S. M., Roberts, G., Vaughan, S., et al. (2007). *Academic literacy instruction for adolescents: A guidance document from the Center on Instruction.* Portsmouth, NH: RMC Research Corporation, Center on Instruction.

This guidance document from the Center on Instruction offers a summary of research conducted in the reading comprehension of adolescents and the instruction that produced positive outcomes. Sections cover instruction in content areas, interventions for students reading below grade level, and literacy development in English language learners.

6 Visual Organizers for Note Taking

After teaching so many students who do not like note taking, but who love drawing, sketching, and doodling, I began to teach some of my students to use their visual talents in a more graphic form of note taking called "mindmapping." I became very concerned because the "maps" of many students were quite confusing, were difficult to understand, and did not produce review systems that were easy to use. Often, the visual display was crowded, the connections were vague, and the organization was loose. For some students, the use of visual strategies such as mindmapping, "spidering," "webbing," or "clustering" is quite helpful, but, for others, the structure is not explicit since the techniques do not display the sequential order and rely heavily on the student's ability to organize the ideas after brainstorming.

To use the positive aspects of visual strategies, but provide more structure related to sequential organization, the strategy called Wheels for Reading was developed. The display is visual, but the sequence will also be displayed in a more linear manner, which is critical for some students.

WHEELS FOR READING

The "Wheels for Reading" strategy uses an oval called a wheel in a column or vertical flow map as an organizational tool for tracking main ideas and details in a more visual display than in traditional note-taking strategies. Wheels are always in a vertical column and never branch sideways so that the sequence (order) is established visually. Within a wheel is a main idea, and related details or information are attached in a spokelike manner around the wheel (e.g., see the Student Example that follows). The approach is very simple.

While reading the material, the student should do the following:

- Draw an oval and put the first main idea (may be the subtitle) in the oval.
- Attach related information around the wheel in a spokelike fashion.
- Draw another oval right underneath the previous wheel for a new idea (may be the next subtitle).
- Write the main idea in the wheel and attach the related information around the wheel.
- Continue the process until the reading has been completed.

Student Sample

The Loch Ness Monster

In Scotland lies a very famous lake called Loch Ness. The lake is about 24 miles long, a mile wide, and approximately 650 feet deep. Overlooking the lake, and adding mystique, are several local castles, including the famous Urquhart Castle and the Aldourie Castle. However, the main attraction is the presence of a large, serpentlike monster named "Nessie."

The Loch Ness Monster may be the most famous sea serpent in the world. It is described as being 40 to 60 feet long with a head about the size of a horse's. Its thin neck is about six feet long and is attached to a fat body with an eight-foot-long tail. The description is similar to a dinosaur known as the plesiosaurus. Scientists think that Nessie is a plesiosaurus who has survived since prehistoric times.

A large number of people have reported seeing Nessie. Alex Campbell was working on the loch when he saw something serpentlike moving in the water. He quit his job immediately. Next, Arthur Grant was riding his motorcycle on the highway that surrounds Loch Ness. He was startled by a huge shape that crossed the road and slid into the water. Arthur turned his bike around and ended his trip. A London surgeon took a picture of a head and neck protruding from the water, but the picture is fuzzy and unclear. Tim Dinsdale took a motion picture of a living creature that was about fifty feet long and positioned on the other side of the loch. Finally, Clem Skelton, a technician with the Loch Ness Phenomena Investigation Bureau, which was established to investigate reported sightings, spotted the monster when he was out on the loch on a boating trip.

The Loch Ness Investigation Bureau has two purposes. The first is the investigation of sightings so that a hoax will not be perpetrated on the world. The second is the organization of searches that will provide additional information about the monster. The most recent searches are very different from the sightings by eye or ordinary camera. The use of equipment such as sonar, underwater cameras, and submarines may result in definitive answers to the questions about the monster that lives in the depths of Loch Ness.

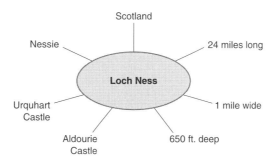

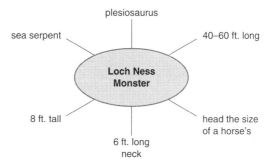

(continued)

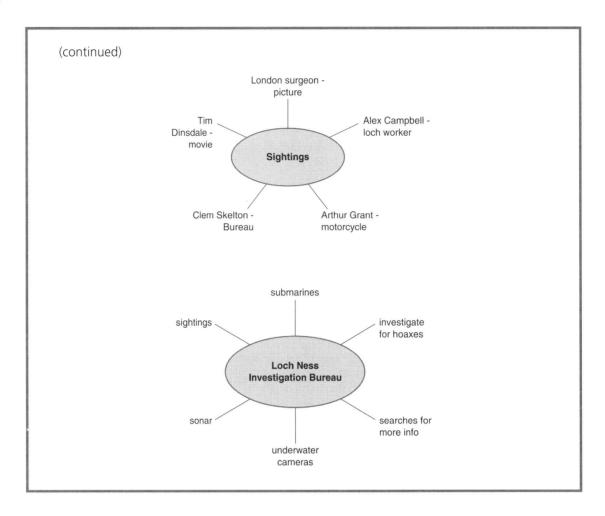

(continued)

A guide for making a new wheel can be the number of items around the wheel, headers, or subtitles. If too many details are being attached to a wheel, the main idea may be too general and should be divided into two ideas. If the detail is no longer related to the main idea in the wheel, a new wheel is made.

Again, guides for the details that have to be attached are names of people and places, important numbers, and terms. Any other important material can be attached as well, but in a "memory jog" style with a minimum number of words. The wheels are always in a linear column, one after the other in a vertical line with no interconnecting of lines or wheels.

The wheels are developed during the initial reading to support comprehension and produce a graphic organizer for efficient review as soon as the reading is completed. For students who have good visualization skills, the visual format of the wheel and spokes is easier to recall from memory than a language presentation. For example, Jonathan, a high school baseball star, could not remember the history he had to learn until he began to use the wheel approach, which clearly identified the main ideas and the details in a visual format he could recall. Since he could "picture" the wheels, he could then answer questions; however, he was not able to retain information presented in paragraph format.

If identifying the main idea is difficult, advise the student to try the first sentence in the paragraph. If that sentence doesn't work, have the student try the last sentence in the paragraph. As a last resort, the student should pick out a major word from the paragraph that can be placed in the wheel as a possible main idea.

After completion of the reading, the student should count the number of items around each of the wheels and record the number inside the wheel. To practice retrieval, the student can put his or her hands over the wheels so that only the inside of the wheel is visible. The information around the wheel is covered so the student has to recall the information from memory, with the number prompting how many pieces of information should be retrieved. The process is then reversed and a finger is placed over the main idea, which must be recalled after reading the information spiked around the wheel.

WHEELS FOR LITERATURE

Wheels for literature can be as complicated as the demands set forth in a book review format (one wheel for each demand), or it may be as simple as putting the assigned question to be considered while reading a piece of literature into a circle and attaching ideas (or their page numbers) that relate to the question.

Titles and authors must always be included. The wheels establish an advance organizer initially to guide processing and support memory, while producing a visual prompt if sufficient information has not been recorded.

If study questions are available, the questions can serve as a self-check on the accuracy of the information placed on the wheels. Each question should be read to make sure the information necessary to answer the question is attached on a wheel. If the information was not recorded, the information must be found and added to the appropriate wheel.

For the general strategy, the student should do the following:

- Draw three wheels.
- Put the words *Characters, Setting,* and *Plot* each in the center of a wheel.
- Attach information in a spokelike manner to the appropriate wheel.

Wheels can be added to include the topics of study guide questions or particular questions the teacher wants the student to answer. Also, a specific set of wheels can be produced by the teacher to guide the student during the reading process.

Student Samples

Wheels for Literature: Short Story

Title: *Mary*
Author: Katherine Mansfield

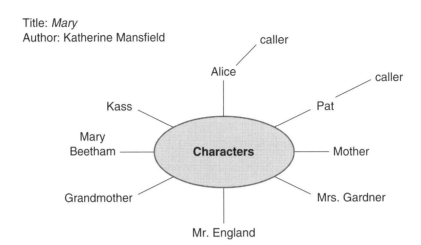

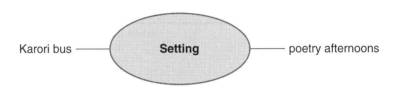

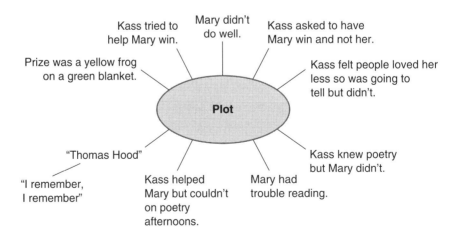

Wheels for Literature: Book With Long Chapters

Title: *A Game of Catch*
Author: Richard Wilbur
Chapter 1

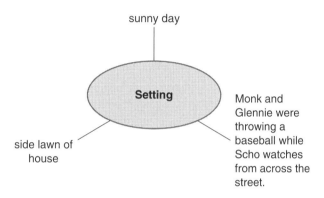

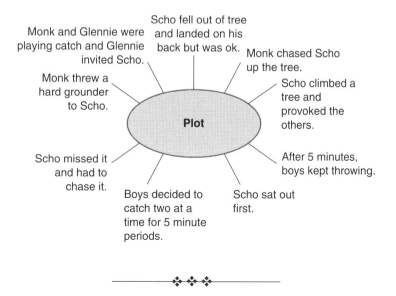

Wheels for Literature: Book With Short Chapters

Title: *David Copperfield*
Author: Charles Dickens

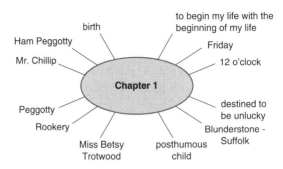

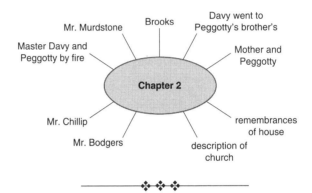

❖ ❖ ❖

Wheels for Literature: Play

Title: *Macbeth*
Author: William Shakespeare

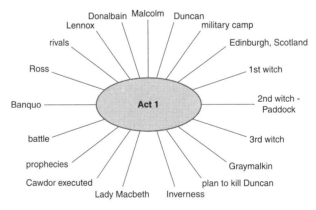

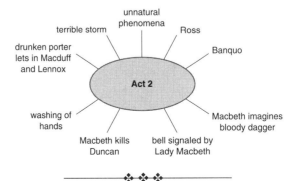

❖ ❖ ❖

Wheels for Literature: Poem

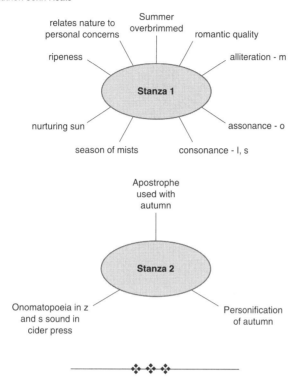

ADDITIONAL RESOURCES

Deshler, D. D., & Schumacker, J. (2005). *Teaching adolescents with disabilities: Accessing the general education curriculum.* Thousand Oaks, CA: Corwin.

This book is written by researchers who investigate learning strategy instruction and present strategies, methods, and guidance to support older students with learning disabilities.

Vaughn, S., & Edmonds, M. (2008). Reading comprehension for older readers. *Intervention in School and Clinic, 41*(3), 131–137.

This article describes the use of graphic organizers such as semantic maps to improve the comprehension of students with learning disabilities.

7 Additional Reading Strategies

LITERATURE GRIDS OR COLUMNS

At times, the use of the wheel approach may not allow for sufficient space, or students may prefer a column or chartlike structure instead. In these formats, a sheet of paper is folded into two columns, or four sections by folding the sheet into a two-column format and then folding again to make squares.

The student should do the following:

- Write *Title* and *Author* at the top of the page.
- Label each section with one of the following labels: *Characters*, *Setting*, *Names*, *Numbers*, and *Plot* (must have a minimum of five entries).
- Fill in the second column or the chart while reading the literature selection.

If the process seems too laborious during the reading, the student can place a check or a "sticky note" strip in the margin to identify information that will need to be added to the chart after the reading.

If study questions are provided, the topics of the questions (reformatting into the topics rather than copying the question) should be written in sections instead of tracking the plot.

Notes are written on the back of the sheet of paper only if the student runs out of room on the front. The categories should always be visible (never on the back of a sheet of paper) to support memory and provide structure during the reading.

Student Sample

Title	"The Dinner Party"
Author	Mona Gardner
Characters	Colonial official Mrs. Wynnes (wife)

	American naturalist Young girl Colonel
Setting	India Dining room Veranda
Names	Mrs. Wynnes Cobra
Numbers	50 rupees 5-minute count 300 count
Plot 1	Argument Servant gets milk Contest
Plot 2	Colonel and young girl disagree about "nerve control"—man versus woman. Colonel says men have more and girl says women do.
Plot 3	American naturalist sees hostess' expression.
Plot 4	Hostess calls servant. Servant places bowl of milk out for cobra. American starts contest to stay still.
Plot 5	Colonel says man had most control. Mrs. Wynnes said snake crawled across her foot. Woman has equal, if not more, nerve control.

NOTATION STRATEGY FOR LITERATURE

Some long assignments, such as plays or novels, which are very involved or complex, may make reading and taking notes simultaneously difficult. Often, students simply read with little attention to the development of a review system, which affects comprehension and future study. The use of notations or notes in the margin can be useful if writing in the book is allowed (the sticky-note strategy is used if writing in the books is not allowed). Make a "key," or list, to use for notations in the margin while reading. For example, character names, setting, events, and actions can be abbreviated by first (or first and second) initials as shown here:

K = Kristen

B = Ben

H = Holden

E = event

S = setting

A = action

The abbreviation is written in the margin (where appropriate) to be used for future review.

MARGIN NOTES

If notes are taken in the margin, the notes should be in a column in the outside margin without having any notes mix with the text. An *x* is placed in the text to identify what the notation refers to or explains. For a student to review, a cover sheet is used to hide the notations, with the *x* identifying the part of the text to be read. After reading the text by the *x*, the student should be able to recall the information in the notation from memory. The process should also be done in reverse by covering the text and recalling the text information while looking at the notation.

These are some notes recorded in the margin from the text.

These are some notes recorded in the margin from the text.

This is the text in the book. This is the text in the book. This is the text in the book. This is the text in the book. This is the text in the book. This is the text in the book. This is the text in the book. This is the text in the book. **X** This is the text in the book. This is the text in the book. This is the text in the book. This is the text in the book. This is the text in the book. This is the text in the book. This is the text in the book. This is the text in the book. This is the text in the book. This is the text in the book. This is the text in the book. This is the text in the book. This is the text in the book. **X** This is the text in the book. This is the text in the book. This is the text in the book. This is the text in the book. This is the text in

---

STICKY-NOTE STRATEGY

If writing is not allowed in the book, sticky notes of different colors should be cut into strips (or strips can be purchased precut). While reading, each strip is placed in the text where important information needs to be identified. The corner of the strip should be placed at the beginning of the important information. After the reading has been completed, a review sheet or notes should be made to list all the information identified by the strips.

PAGE NOTE TAKING

An alternative to the use of sticky notes involves simply taking notes by recording the page and paragraph numbers of important information on a sheet of paper (for example, *67, 3* would mean page 67, paragraph 3). The note taking serves as a map back to important parts of the text and can be used to produce a review sheet or complete a literature chart (see literature grid at the beginning of the chapter) after the reading has been completed.

ADDITIONAL RESOURCES

Reid, R., & Lienemann, T. O. (2006). *Strategy instruction for students with learning disabilities: What works for special needs learners.* New York: Guilford Press.

This book presents practical cognitive strategies for content areas with examples and includes lesson plans.

Strangman, N., Hall, T., & Meyer, A. (2003). *Graphic organizers with UDL.* Wakefield, MA: National Center on Accessing the General Curriculum. Retrieved May 29, 2008, from http://www.cast.org/publications/ncac/ncac_goudl.html

This Web site report summarizes some of the research on the use of graphic organizers during instruction, presents a variety of graphic organizers, and lists related Web sites that may be of interest.

Part II

Note Taking
When Listening

8 Note Taking During Oral Instruction or Lecture

When I think of note taking while information is being presented orally in class, I hear my students saying, "I can listen or take notes, but I can't do both!" Students with memory weaknesses, writing problems, or problems with attention may have more trouble taking notes than would be expected at the secondary level. Often, students are used to teachers putting the notes on the board so they can just copy the information in a rote manner, which does not develop note-taking skills. Instead, students should be taught (and then encouraged to practice) explicit note-taking strategies that support memory and minimize demands on writing.

This chapter describes three basic note-taking strategies and a reduced note-taking strategy that can provide explicit structure to guide note taking during classroom instruction.

STREAMLINED NOTE TAKING (FOR LECTURE)

The streamlined note-taking strategy is designed to provide a running record of the material being presented orally. The emphasis during note taking is on getting information down on paper in some form to provide a record or reminder of what went on during class. If something is presented, but not understood, the student should make any notes possible and use a question mark to identify faulty sections in the notes (or just a question mark can be recorded to identify missing information); the information can then be obtained from someone else's notes, from the teacher, or from a textbook as soon as possible after class. The importance of marking the "trouble spot" where information is missing, or inaccurate, cannot be overemphasized since many students may not remember that the information is faulty or missing after a time delay.

If daydreaming or inattention occurs during a lecture, note taking should be increased to help maintain attention. If information has been missed, boundaries on the lapses in attention should be set by placing a question mark between the last piece of information that was recorded and the piece of information that was being presented when attention was restored.

The second phase of streamlined note taking deals with processing the information in the notes. Note taking without review is not sufficient. The written record must be reviewed, organized, and processed into memory. The notes should be reviewed as soon as possible after they are taken by making up possible test questions for the topics; the questions will serve as a practice test during the study process.

To use streamlined note taking, the student should do the following:

- Fold a sheet of paper in half lengthwise and place a key (list) of abbreviations for words that will be repeated frequently during the presentation (e.g., during a lecture on note taking, the key may contain the abbreviations *n = notes, note taker* and *s = speaker*). Words may be added to the key throughout the lecture. The purpose is to minimize writing demands.

- Place a number *1* in the left-hand margin of the first column to identify the first main idea the speaker presents. The student should think of the lecture as being a conversation and just listen for changes in the topics of conversation. The student records any information about the first topic by simply listing words or ideas under the topic written after the number *1*. If some information is missed or not heard accurately, a question mark is placed by the material or the blank to identify a trouble area.

- Place a number *2* in the margin of the first column and write the new topic when there is a change in topic or the pieces of information don't seem to fit the topic under number *1*. Any information about the second topic is listed under the topic written by the number *2*. The student continues to note changes in topics by placing the next consecutive number in the margin and writing the new topic next to it. If a speaker returns to a previous topic temporarily, the number can simply be picked up again to identify that the previous topic is being discussed.

- Open the sheet completely as soon as possible after the notes have been taken so both columns are visible. In the second column (across from each number in the left column), the student makes up a question for each numbered topic on the left half. The question should be the most difficult one that can be made and should encompass the information listed under the topic. The goals of the question making are the ability to predict questions while integrating the details with the main idea or topic, to support processing into long-term memory, and to produce cumulative tests to practice retrieval of the information from memory.

- Place a big *X* in the left-hand margin when information is missed or not understood so that a textbook, another person, or another source can be used to obtain the needed instruction, information, or clarification before a test.

The note taking results in two columns. In the first column is the information presented during class. In the second column, the predicted questions produce a practice test that should be used when reviewing notes by folding the sheet back so that only the question column is visible; the questions should then be answered, resulting in a practice-test review of notes to make sure retrieval is fluent.

The following guidelines will make question making more successful:

- If making a question is difficult (which indicates a lack of comprehension), a request for additional instruction should be made.
- When the notes have question marks, a big *X* should be placed in the left-hand margin so that the trouble spot is clearly marked. Before the next class or test, the correct information should be obtained from the teacher, textbook, or other source of information, such as a Web site.
- If the notes contain pieces that don't seem accurate, the accuracy should be checked by comparing the notes with another person's notes.

Though the most common method of reviewing notes is to "read over" or "highlight" them, recalling the information from memory without support (such as during a test) may be problematic. For example, Maria was distraught because she knew the information, but she could not recall what she had studied during the test. However, two hours after the test, she might remember the answer or the information she needed to recall during the test, which did not help. Comments such as "I know it, but I can't remember it now," "It's on the tip of my tongue," or "I can see it in my notes, but I can't remember it!" all reflect retrieval problems that have not been accommodated in the study process.

A tape or computer-based recorder can be helpful as a tool to support note taking. However, the recorder should not be used instead of note taking; rather it can be helpful to fill in information when reviewing the notes.

Streamlined Note Taking: Example 1

Key

New England = NE

Puritans = P

Massachusetts = M

1. Three regions
    NE
    Middle colonies
    Southern colonies
	1. What were the three regions of New World colonies?

2. NE colonies
    New Hampshire
    Connecticut?
    Rhode Island
    M
	2. What were the NE colonies?

3. 1620: P
    Religious
    Strict
    Pure
    ?
	3. What were the characteristics of the P?

4. Dissenters
    Disagree with Church of England
    Called Separatists
	4. What was another name for P?

Streamlined Note Taking: Example 2

Key

RS = Respiratory system

O_2 = Oxygen

CO_2 = Carbon dioxide

1. Trachea Air through bronchi	1. How does air flow through bronchial tubes into air sacs?
2. Nose and mouth Goes to trachea and then bronchial tubes; then lungs or air sacs—oxygen and carbon dioxide exchange	2. Describe the path.
3. Cilia Little hairs in bronchi and trachea	3. Define cilia.

4. RS supplies blood with O_2
    Inhale O_2, exhale CO_2
    Exchange of gasses puts O_2 in blood
    Nose, mouth, lungs, trachea, diaphragm
    Nose and mouth take in air
    Trachea: tube into chest, become two bronchi, pass into lungs
    O_2 passes into alveoli and goes into blood by capillaries
    Diaphragm: pump
    Waste makes CO_2
    Exhale: CO_2 out the same way
	4. How does the RS work?

5. Air sacs called alveoli About 600 million in lungs Spongy and full of air Surrounded by capillaries	5. What happens in the air sacs?
6. Air breathed is clean Mucus Hair in nose Trachea and bronchi Cilia	6. How is the air you breathe cleaned?

TWO-COLUMN NOTE TAKING (FOR USE IN CONTENT-AREA SUBJECTS)

When taking notes in content-area classes, using a note-taking procedure that isolates details and tracks related information in a bulleted list may be very helpful to support test preparation. With this strategy, the names, numbers, terms, and topics are written in the first column with the related information listed in the second column, producing a retrieval-practice study system right from the start of the note taking. Rather than having to reorganize notes into a better study system, the use of isolation and a two-column format produces a system that facilitates frequent review using retrieval practice. The notes are taken in the double columns and are reviewed by folding the paper so that only one column is visible. While looking at the name, number, term, or topic, the student has to recall from memory the related information in the hidden column. Then, the student turns the columns and retrieves the name, number, term, or topic that is related to the information in the visible column.

The student should do the following:

- Divide the sheet of paper into two columns by folding the paper in half lengthwise or drawing a line down the center of the paper.
- List the specific information (names, numbers, terms, and topics) in the first column.
- Write the definitions, explanations, or related information using a list format in the second column across from the name, number, term, topic, or question in the first column.

To review the information, the sheet is folded so that only one column is visible, and the information in the hidden column is retrieved from memory. The columns are then reversed, and the hidden column information is recalled from memory.

By using both columns, specific retrieval practice and integration with concepts are supported. The process actually results in "practice tests," which are more efficient than "reading over notes."

The strategy supports attention, processing, and retrieval in the study process.

Sample

Names, Numbers, Terms, Topics	Related Information
August 9, 1974	Nixon resigned
White House Horrors	Crimes
Democratic National Committee (DNC) Headquarters	Place of break-in
Watergate break-in	1. Illegal microphones 2. "Bugs" 3. Photos of documents
May 28, 1972	1st break-in
Moscow	Where Nixon was
Five men	Broke in
Watergate office	Place
Howard Johnson's	Intelligence equipment
E. Howard Hunt	CIA and aide
G. Gordon Liddy	FBI and Council for Re-Election
First break-in	1. Five men did it. 2. Espionage operation 3. Two men planned
John Dean	Counsel: handles Hunt's hush money
November, 1972	Conspiracy
IRS	Illegal operations
Enemies list	IRS
Cancer of the presidency	Dean's testimony
Conspiracy	1. Break-ins 2. Hush money 3. Dean: bagman for blackmail 4. Crumbled with Dean's testimony

REDUCED NOTE TAKING

Reduced note taking is a form of note taking designed for students who have great difficulty listening to orally presented material while trying to record the information in writing. This strategy makes a record of the topics, names, terms, or numbers, without taking notes on all the related information. Using the two-column format, the topics, names, terms, and numbers are recorded in the left column with some white space around each item, leaving the right column blank. The notes provide a skeleton of the material (or review sheet) that can be used to make sure all the details and topics presented during class are included in notes taken when the reading was assigned. Taking notes during reading allows the student to work at his or her own pace, have visual support, and use the textbook format to serve as a guide. If any name, number, term, or topic is not included in the notes taken while reading, notes on the detail or topic should be taken in the second column. The student may obtain the missing information from other students, the teacher, the textbook, or related Web sites.

The strategy supports attention, reduces writing demands, and minimizes gaps in the set of notes. The student does not have to look up all the details and topics presented during class since most of them will be covered during the assigned reading. Therefore, only those that were taken in class and were not in the reading require additional notes.

The systems, which are cumulative, are reviewed using the flash card study approach or hiding one of the columns from view while retrieving the information from memory.

The minimal writing during the listening phase reduces the processing demands while emphasizing the topics, names, terms, or numbers, which supports focus of attention. This strategy tells students specifically what to listen for, does not rely on making judgments about the importance of the information, and reduces the writing demands.

List Topics, Names, Terms and Numbers	Add Information After Oral Presentation (from a textbook or other person's notes)
Organizational learning strategies	
Visual anchors	
White space	

List Topics, Names, Terms and Numbers	*Add Information After Oral Presentation (from a textbook or other person's notes)*
Isolation	
Wheels versus mindmapping	

If the student has done note taking from the textbook, only the names, numbers, terms, and topics not found in the reading notes need to have information added.

ADDITIONAL RESOURCES

Boyle, J. (2006). Learning from lecture: The implications of notetaking for students with learning disabilities. *Learning Disabilities: A Multi-Disciplinary Journal, 14*(2), 91–97.

This article describes students with learning disabilities as being ineffective note takers who often have incomplete or minimal notes and presents strategies to improve their note-taking skills when listening to lecture-style instruction.

Lenz, B. K., & Deshler, D. D. (2004). *Teaching content to all: Evidence-based inclusive practices in middle and secondary schools.* Boston: Allyn & Bacon.

This book addresses diversity at the secondary level, presents evidence-based learning strategies, and links the strategies to content instruction.

9 Additional Note-Taking Strategies

NOTE TAKING FROM VISUALS (BLACKBOARD, PROJECTOR, OR POWERPOINT)

First Strategy

When material is presented visually and not orally, the information should be taken down exactly as it is displayed; however, the information should be loaded into a column rather than spread across the page so the second column can be used to predict test questions and serve as a practice test in the study process. For example, the following notes were on the blackboard to be copied upon entering class:

The Last Days of Pompeii: AD 79

Vesuvius overflowed and buried 2,000 people in the city.

City was a "frozen portrait."

Excavation enabled modern man to look at Pompeii.

Plan of the city described lifestyle.

Public buildings and the Forum were important parts of the city.

Student Sample

The Last Days of Pompeii: AD 79 Vesuvius overflowed and buried 2,000 people in the city. City was a "frozen portrait."	Describe the last days of Pompeii.
Excavation enabled modern man to look at Pompeii. Plan of the city described lifestyle. Public buildings and the Forum were important parts of the city.	Summarize the importance of Pompeii.

Second Strategy

An alternative strategy that can be employed during class is the use of the two-column format to reformat the information on the board, overhead projector, or PowerPoint presentation by having the student copy the names, numbers, terms, and topics into the first column and write the related information in the second column. For example, the following notes were on the blackboard to be copied upon entering class:

The Last Days of Pompeii: AD 79

Vesuvius overflowed and buried 2,000 people in the city.

City was a "frozen portrait."

Excavation enabled modern man to look at Pompeii.

Plan of the city described lifestyle.

Public buildings and the Forum were important parts of the city.

Student Sample

Pompeii	
AD 79	
Vesuvius	1. Overflowed 2. Buried city
2,000	People killed
Frozen portrait	1. Excavation enabled modern man to look at Pompeii. 2. Plan of the city described lifestyle.
Forum	Public buildings and Forum were important parts of the city.

During the study process, the paper is folded so that only the first column is visible and the second column has to be retrieved from memory; the process is then reversed.

Third Strategy

A third strategy is to leave space between the main sections being copied. Later, test questions should be made up to process the information or to relate the notes to other information from lectures or textbooks.

The notes should be taken like this:

The Last Days of Pompeii: AD 79

Vesuvius overflowed and buried 2,000 people in the city.

City was a "frozen portrait."

Excavation enabled modern man to look at Pompeii.

Plan of the city described lifestyle.

Public buildings and the Forum were important parts of the city.

Later, the blanks should be filled in with test questions as in the example below:

The Last Days of Pompeii: AD 79

Vesuvius overflowed and buried 2,000 people in the city
City was a "frozen portrait."

Describe the last days of Pompeii.

Excavation enabled modern man to look at Pompeii.
Plan of the city described lifestyle.
Public buildings and the Forum were important parts of the city.

Compare the city plan of Pompeii with a modern city in terms of how the peoples' lifestyle affected the buildings' architecture and layout of the cities.

The use of a sheet of paper as a cover sheet is recommended when studying. The student should use a sheet of paper to cover the answer while looking at the question. The student should then retrieve the answer from memory. As a second step, the student can cover the question with the sheet of paper and recall the topic of the question while looking at the answer.

Fourth Strategy

Another strategy is the use of the note-taking-without-subtitles strategy, using the notes as the text to produce a flash card review system that isolates details and concepts and develops a specific retrieval system. The cards can be made as a homework assignment that requires the student to reformat, reorganize, and review the notes from class that day.

WHEELS FOR NOTE TAKING

Wheels that are used to take notes when reading or when organizing writing can also be used for note taking. The student should place the general topic or date at the top of the page and draw a wheel (oval). The first idea presented is put in the wheel, and the related information is attached around it. When the second idea is presented, a wheel is drawn underneath the first wheel, and the idea is put inside the wheel with related information around the wheel. The process is continued until the lecture is over; then the items around each wheel are counted and the number is written inside the wheel. To study the information, the student's hands are placed around the wheel so that only the inside of the wheel is visible; the number identifies the number of pieces of information related to the topic that should be recalled from memory. Unknown information should be reviewed. The process should be reversed by covering the center of the wheel and retrieving the topic or main idea from the items attached to the outside of the wheel. See the following examples.

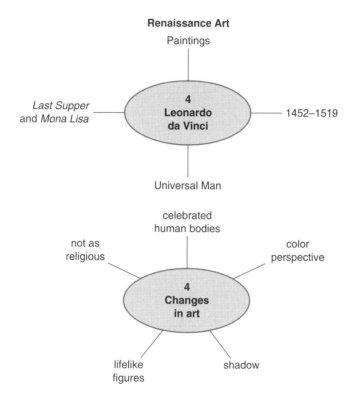

NOTE-TAKING GRID ADVANCE ORGANIZER

Prior to listening in class, a grid can be set up to support note taking by using the textbook.

The teacher can set up grids by using the identification items or questions at the end of the chapter to identify names, numbers, terms, and topics to provide visual support to guide note taking.

Identification Items

Citizen, Representative, Alien, Office of Citizen

Discussion Questions

1. Describe the process to become a U.S. citizen.
2. Explain naturalization.
3. What are the rights associated with citizenship?

Grid

Topic: Citizen	Topic: Representative
Information:	Information:
Topic: Alien	Topic: Office of Citizen
Information:	Information:
Topic: Qualifications	Topic: Naturalization
Information:	Information:
Topic: Rights	
Information:	

Alternate Strategy

The same process can be done using wheels instead of grids. Each identification item or topic is placed in a wheel, and the notes are attached to the appropriate wheel during class.

USING PICTORIALS DURING NOTE TAKING

For students who find themselves "thinking in pictures" or doodling while listening, the use of pictorials can be incorporated into note taking by using the following strategy.

The student should do the following:

- Fold a sheet of paper in half to form two columns.
- Take notes in the first column by making a pictorial to act as an "anchor" for words, phrases, or information to be recorded.
- The picture establishes the concept in a visual manner, and words are added as appropriate. After the class is over, the student uses the second column for review by adding information on the topic, by looking up the topic in a textbook in order to add detail to the notes, or by changing the information in the picture into a verbal list.

Student Sample

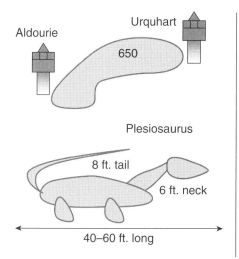

Loch Ness - lake in Scotland
surrounded by castles
(Urquhart and Aldourie)

Nessie is thought to be a
plesiosaurus 40–60 ft. long,
with a head like horse,
8 ft. tail, and 6 ft. neck.

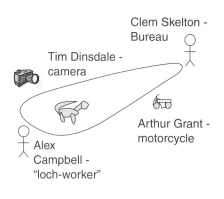

4 sightings:
Tim Dinsdale - camera
Alex Campbell - loch-worker
Arthur Grant - motorcycle
Clem Skelton - Bureau

Loch Ness Bureau

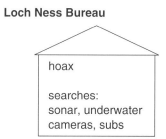

Loch Ness Phenomena
Investigation Bureau

1. Stop hoaxes
2. Search for truth with sonar,
   underwater cameras, and
   submarines

USING PICTORIALS AFTER NOTE TAKING

The student should do the following:

- Fold a sheet of paper in half to form two columns.
- Take notes by writing the number *1* and recording the information presented about the first topic.
- Write the number *2* when the topic changes and record information about the topic.
- Continue the process until the class has ended.

After class, in the second column, the student should do the following:
- Review the notes by moving the numbers representing the topics into the second column.
- Read the information on the topic and make a pictorial or diagram representing the information in the second column to deepen processing and provide visual display.

Student Sample

1. 3 tools

wheels
rectangles
cards

2. Wheels

visual display
depict main ideas and details
   clearly
must be in a line or column
not like mindmapping, clustering,
   spidering, or webbing
   organizationally

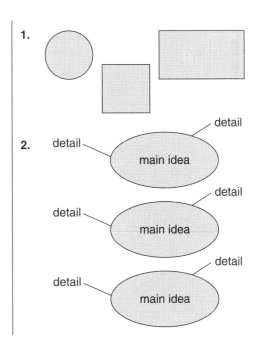

3. Rectangles

note taking
concept squares
correction squares

4. Cards

specific retrieval
card sort process
flash card study
isolation of detail

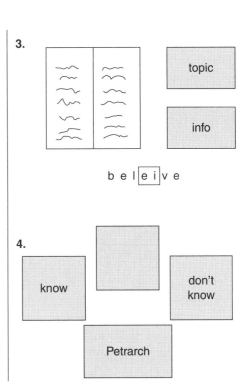

NOTE TAKING DURING MATH CLASS

Often, notes from math class consist of examples completed with very little verbal explanation of the topic, process, or type of problem. More extensive note taking using a two-column format should make a record of the verbal instruction, develop self-talk procedures, and rephrase the steps in the process during math class.

The student should do the following:

- Divide the paper into two columns, with the first column being the widest one.
- Write the concept, topic, or type of problem that is being taught in the first column.
- Record the examples or problems being taught in the first, wider column.
- Write a verbal explanation, summary of steps, or definition of terminology in the second column across from the example or type of problem.

While looking at the concept, topic, or example, the student recalls the explanation or the steps in the process and then turns the paper so that only the second column is visible. From the explanation or description of the steps in the process, the student identifies the type of problem and the concept or topic.

Example, Concept, Topic	*Explanation or Process*
Single Variable Equations	
$2x + 4 = 28$ $2x = 24$ $x = 12$	1. Subtract 4 from both sides of the original equation, giving $2x = 24$. 2. Divide both sides of the equation by 2. 3. The final answer $x = 12$.
	General Process
$4x + 16 = 48$ $\underline{-16 \quad -16}$ $4x = 32$ $4x \div 4 = 32 \div 4$ $x = 8$	1. Subtract the constant from both sides of the equation if the number is a plus. 2. Divide both sides by the number in front of the unknown. 3. Unknown is by itself so the number is the answer.

REORGANIZATION OF NOTES AFTER CLASS

If notes are not organized during the note taking, reorganizing the notes can be a good way to review as well as make a review system, but it is more time-consuming. The student should divide a sheet of paper into two columns by folding it lengthwise in half or drawing a line down the center of the paper lengthwise. In the first column, the specific information that will need to be recalled is listed. Specific information includes names (proper, not common, nouns), numbers, terms, and topics. A term is a word that needs to be learned so that vocabulary building in the content area takes place and is not limited to the bold-print words in the text. The specific information needs to be isolated (surrounded by white space) to support focus of attention.

In the second column, the definitions, explanations, or related information are written across from the name, number, topic, or term.

Example of Notes

Italian Renaissance 1400–1600

Renaissance can be defined as the rebirth of Greek and Roman culture. Rebirth took place in Western Europe. The Renaissance began in Northern Italy and gradually spread through most of Europe.

Renaissance was a product of urban society, and the city of Florence was the undisputed capital of the period (Pisa, Milan, Florence, Genoa, Venice). The reasons for the tremendous cultural rebirth of Europe are the following:

a. Emphasis on literacy brought about by the revival of commerce in the 14th century.

b. Most books that were written only in Latin were now written in the vernacular, or spoken language of a particular area, giving everyone a chance to read and write.

Renaissance brought a growth of the middle class caused by a revival in trade. The middle class to a large extent sponsored writers and artists, giving them a chance to develop their skills. The increase in wealth caused people to think more about acquiring wealth and less about religion and the church. The Medici family funded, or sponsored, artists in Florence.

Growth of the Renaissance was aided by the end of feudalism and brought about the rise of the middle class and the fall of the nobility. It opened society and allowed people to seek knowledge.

Growth of the Renaissance was also aided by the invention of the printing press around 1450 by John Gutenburg. It definitely increased the availability of books and reduced their cost.

Renaissance—another important factor was the growth of humanism started by Mirandola in his book *On the Dignity of Man*. In the book, Mirandola said that each man should enjoy a full, rich life on earth and not be so concerned about death and eternity. Humanists believed that man was good and that God served as the ultimate judge but did not interfere in the workings of the earth.

Reorganized Notes

Names, Numbers, Terms, Topics	Related Information
Italian Renaissance	Rebirth
1400–1600	When
Greek and Roman	Cultures revived

Names, Numbers, Terms, Topics	Related Information
Northern Italy	Where began
Florence	Capital
Pisa	Urban city
Milan	Urban city
Genoa	Urban city
Venice	Urban city
Literary	More people could read and write
14th century	Commerce revived
Latin	Language books were in
Vernacular	Spoken language
Middle class	Grew More wealth Less religion
Medici	Family who sponsored writers and artists
Feudalism	Caste system
1450	Printing press
John Gutenburg	Invented printing press
Humanism	Man: good God: judge No divine interference
Mirandola	Author
On the Dignity of Man	Book: enjoy life

To review the information, the student folds the sheet so only one column is visible and recalls the information in the second column from memory. The student then turns the paper so that only the second column is visible and recalls the information in the first column from memory.

ADDITIONAL RESOURCES

AdLit.org. *All about Adolescent Literacy. Resources for parents and educators of kids in grades 4–12.*

This Web site is an initiative of WETA, a public television and radio station in Washington, D.C., with funding by the Carnegie Foundation of New York and the Ann B.

and Thomas L. Friedman Family Foundation. It is an excellent resource for a wide range of topics, strategies, and interventions for older students.

Boyle, J. R. (2001). Enhancing the notetaking skills of students with mild disabilities. *Intervention in School and Clinic, 36*(4), 221–224.

This article describes ways to improve the performance of students by improving their note-taking skills.

WETA-TV Web sites: LD Online.org, ReadingRockets.org, and ColorinColorado.org.

These are Web sites sponsored by WETA, a public television and radio station in Washington, D.C., and are tremendous resources for parents and teachers. The Web sites are related to learning disabilities with reading and learning English.

Part III
Language Arts

10 Decoding and Spelling

Helping the older student develop decoding skills can be a challenge. Though word-level skills such as decoding and spelling (encoding) are taught in lower grade levels and assumed to be fluent skills by high school, remediation of decoding and spelling needs to be available at the secondary level. Instruction that is structured, systematic, explicit, and reiterative should be provided to improve the word-level literacy skills of students who have not developed those skills (see *Resources* for a list of programs that provide remediation). Helping students who can't read proficiently to pass classes and complete graduation requirements without remediation to develop their literacy skills produces "graduates" who can't read well. Teachers with the appropriate professional preparation should provide remediation. The strategies in this chapter do not take the place of remediation; however, a teacher may share these strategies to help students break words into segments to support *word attack* and spelling skills for words in particular content areas.

DECODING

Any word list can be used for this strategy. The words can be from the content area, can be a personalized list based on common words the student should be able to decode easily, or can be basic grade-level vocabulary words that need to be learned. The student makes cards (or uses a column format) on which he or she writes the following:

- The whole word
- The word in parts
- The whole word again

The definition can be put on the back of the card if vocabulary development is part of the instruction. Otherwise, the strategy produces a set of cards that the student uses to practice decoding the words.

For example, if the word is *belligerent*, the card may look like this:

```
belligerent

bell  iger  ent

belligerent
```

The student should read the whole word, read the word in parts, and then reread the whole word. The strategy can be used as part of the general curriculum to develop stronger word attack and segmentation skills.

SPELLING

Good spellers are usually at a loss to describe their excellent spelling abilities. The usual comment is that they "just know" how to spell a word. Most good spellers use a combination approach; they don't have a "way" of spelling, but they probably have several ways to remember the correct spelling.

The spelling strategy does not replace spelling instruction, but it does provide a structured method to process words using a variety of approaches (multisensory). The strategy should be used to learn spelling words, content area terms, or vocabulary words; however, the use of the strategy should also be applied to written production by keeping a spelling file of the words that are misspelled frequently. These words should be organized into a flash card system for daily review so the words can be learned to an automatic level. The flashcard system can also be made into a "personal" spelling reference list to reduce practicing misspellings. Words that are identified by a spell-check computer program may be a good source of words that need to be learned.

The strategy uses index cards so that a cumulative spelling file can be maintained. On the front of the card, the student should do the following:

- Write the correct spelling of the word.
- Spell the word out loud.
- Spell and write the word in parts.
- Mark visual clues such as small words within the word.

Then, the student turns the card over and does the following:

- Writes the word from memory.
- Marks the visual clues again.
- Writes the word with eyes closed.

The card file will serve as an individualized spelling dictionary and help review the correct spelling of the words learned.

If done with the column format, the first column acts as the front of the card and the second column acts as the back of the card.

If done on a computer, the page is divided into three columns, placing the correct spelling of the word in the first column, dividing the word into parts in the second column, and typing the word with eyes closed in the third column.

If words will be dictated on a spelling test, writing the words from dictation should be part of the study practice. The student can tape the words in order to practice dictation independently.

Student Sample: Cards

(front of card)	(back of card)
believe	believe
be lie ve	believe (eyes closed)

(front of card)	(back of card)
miserable	miserable
mis er able	miserable (eyes closed)

(front of card)	(back of card)
belligerent	belligerent
bell iger ent	belligerent (eyes closed)

Student Sample: Two-Column Format

Believe	believe
be lie ve	believe (eyes closed)
Miserable	miserable
mis er able	miserable (eyes closed)
Belligerent	belligerent
bell iger ent	belligerent (eyes closed)

ADDITIONAL RESOURCES

National Reading Panel. (2000). *Teaching children to read: An evidence-based assessment of the scientific research literature on reading and its implications for reading instruction.* Washington, DC: National Institute of Child Health and Human Development.

The National Reading Panel was charged with reviewing the research on reading instruction to determine the critical components of successful literacy instruction and has been used as a guide to develop and assess interventions.

Viel-Ruma, K., Houchins, D., & Frederick, L. (2007). Error self-correction and spelling: Improving the spelling accuracy of secondary students with disabilities in written expression. *Journal of Behavioral Education, 16*(3), 291–301.

This study targets spelling instruction at the secondary level, which is an area needing much more attention and research with older students.

11 English Grammar

For many students, grammar is a problem from first grade right through senior year of high school. If students are asked about grammar, they will often say that they know the parts of speech, but their performance on grammar tests reflects a lack of understanding of how language functions. Recognition of grammatical structures does not necessarily indicate comprehension of the underlying concepts that support use, application, and generalization. Students need to understand the function of parts of speech, punctuation, and rules of syntax.

Some of my students develop their own rules that work often enough to let them pass a grammar quiz, but they do not understand the true operational rule. For example, when Jonathan had to identify the subject and verb in sentences on his grammar quiz, he shared that he discovered the subject was often the second or third word in the sentence, and the verb was either the next word or was very close, which enabled him to get a passing grade, though he did not really understand the concepts of subject or verb. The rule worked enough that the lack of comprehension was not readily apparent, but the skill could not translate into improved reading or writing.

Concept or rule cards require the student to isolate the topic, rephrase the rule or concept, and apply the learned concept without assistance. The student must produce an example to make sure the concept is understood and can be applied. The examples are corrected so "careless errors" are identified to reduce their occurrence in the future, particularly on tests. The cards produce a review system that facilitates frequent review to develop automaticity.

After the concept or rule has been taught in class, the cards are made from the instructional section of a grammar textbook, from handouts, or from class notes. The students are taught to isolate the topic on one side of the card, take notes from the instructional sections on the back, and, when the book/notes have an example, produce an original example on the card without any assistance (such as looking at the book or asking another person). The cards are checked for accuracy. If the student can't make an example, the student needs extended instruction until he or she can produce an original example that is correct. The cards should be reviewed frequently to develop automaticity.

The cards are a great homework assignment after a topic has been presented in class. The cards will identify students who need more instruction and correct application errors prior to the test.

Research has shown that grammar instruction should be embedded within language contexts, so the use of the cards should be incorporated within the context of reading and writing; the cards can be helpful to increase the intensity of the initial instruction and support frequent review.

Two basic types of cards are recommended. The first card simply isolates the rule on the front of the card and requires production of an example that forces application on the back of the card so comprehension can be checked and errors corrected.

CONCEPT OR RULE CARDS: OPTION ONE

A concept or rule is written on the front of an index card with an example produced on the back of the card. The example is corrected, and corrections remain on the card to focus attention on errors when reviewing the cards in the future to reduce careless errors.

<table>
<tr>
<td>

(front of card)

    Prepositional Phrases

    Adjective phrases tell about nouns or pronouns.

    Adverb phrases tell about verbs.

    Same phrase can act as both.

</td>
<td>

(back of card)

    Adjective phrase: The girl in the park ran.

    Adverb phrase: The girl ran in the park.

</td>
</tr>
</table>

While looking at the example, the student should retrieve the concept or rule that is on the hidden side of the card. The cards should be reviewed frequently, if not daily, using the card-sort process by dividing cards into *sure* and *not sure* piles.

CONCEPT OR RULE CARDS: OPTION TWO

The second type of card isolates the topic, concept, or rule on the front of the card, with the explanation and example on the back of the card. The student should do the following:

- Write the topic or rule on the front of the card.
- Draw a line across the back of the card, producing two sections.
- Take notes in the top section (notes may be taken from the instructional section of a book or class notes).
- Produce an original example in the bottom section without any assistance (such as looking back at the examples in the book).
- Have the notes and examples checked for accuracy so errors are corrected and remain on the card as warnings to increase awareness of

careless errors and reduce their occurrence on tests. The cards should be reviewed frequently, possibly daily, by looking at the topic, concept, or rule and recalling the explanation to develop automaticity.

| (front of card)

adverb phrase | (back of card)
 1. prepositional phrase that tells about a verb.
 2. tells when, where, or how action of verb takes place.

 1. The girl ran in the park.
 2. The girl ran in the park.
 The girl ran in the morning.
 The girl ran ~~quickly~~ with speed. |

PERSONAL REVIEW JOURNAL

The following organizer can be used by students to develop "user-friendly" review books (journals) from English grammar textbooks, handouts, or class notes.

The advance organizer below should be done in a review notebook (or grammar file on a computer) or at the end of the class notes whenever a new topic is presented. The journal can be an excellent homework assignment after instruction to make sure the student has understood the instruction.

Using the textbook, handouts, or class notes, the student should do the following:

- Isolate the concept at the top of a page.
- Take notes using the instructional sections in the book, a handout, or class notes.
- Make an original example whenever the student sees an example in the text (the provided example should be hidden from view by using a cover sheet or turning the material over so the examples are out of sight). Reliance on the provided model should be eliminated; many times, dependence on the model occurs even if there is no intent to do so. This enables students to complete homework assignments, but results in trouble on tests, which do not provide any models.
- Have the notes and examples checked for accuracy, and have errors highlighted, corrected, and allowed to remain to forewarn students about these areas during subsequent study while preparing for tests.

This format is outlined as follows:

Topic: The topic is often at the top of the page or section or may be in a different size or color print.

Notes: The notes are taken whenever something is being taught and are rephrased.

Example: The example should be original, without any opportunity to see the models.

Errors: The errors are any corrections made to the examples, predicted errors, or errors made on a test.

If the book or notes return to instruction, then notes are taken again by repeating the label *Notes* and rephrasing the instruction from the book until examples are given again. When examples are given, the student repeats the label *Example*, covers the books/notes, and produces original examples of what has been taught.

There will be as many sections of notes and examples as the textbook, notes, or handout has, and there will be only one *Topic* section.

The organizer should be done on each topic presented in class or assigned for study so that the resulting notebook or section following the class notes will allow for a fast review of the topic, the instruction, and the potential errors. Attention will be focused on errors that are clarified in the study process rather than by failure on a test.

Student Sample: Text From Grammar Book, Handout, or Notes

Prepositional Phrases as Adjective and Adverb Phrases

Prepositional phrases can do the work of adjectives in telling more about nouns or do the work of adverbs in telling more about verbs.

An adjective phrase tells about a noun or pronoun. For example, The dog *by the tree* was wagging its tail. The phrase tells what dog is referred to in the sentence.

An adverb phrase tells about the verb. For example, The cat jumped *into the tree*. The phrase tells about the action of the verb.

The same prepositional phrase may work as an adjective or adverb phrase.

Adjective phrase: The girl in the pool was swimming.

Adverb phrase: The girl was swimming in the pool.

In the first sentence, the phrase tells about the girl so it is an adjective phrase, but in the second sentence the phrase tells where the girl is swimming so the phrase is an adverb phrase.

Student Sample From Textbook

Topic: Prepositional phrases as adjectives or adverbs

Notes: Adjective prepositional phrase

Tells about noun or pronoun

Example: The boy ran home. Correction: The boy in the park ran home. There must be a prepositional phrase.

Notes: Adverb prepositional phrase

Tells about verb

Example: The girl ran to the store.

Notes: Prepositional phrase can be either adjective or adverb—can tell usage by how it is used and where it is in the sentence.

Examples: Adjective: The girl in the park ran. Adverb: The girl ran in the park.

ADDITIONAL RESOURCES

Baker, S., Gersten, R., & Graham, S. (2003). Teaching expressive writing to students with learning disabilities: Research-based applications and examples. *Journal of Learning Disabilities, 36*(2), 109–115.

This is a good example of translating research to practice and is strengthened by the use of examples.

Mastropieri, M. A., & Scruggs, T. E. (2007). *The inclusive classroom: Strategies for effective instruction* (3rd ed.). Columbus, OH: Prentice Hall/Merrill.

This book presents a wide selection of strategies in the context of collaboration, inclusive settings, higher incidence disabilities, lower incidence disabilities, and diverse special needs.

Writing 12

Writing can be problematic in terms of production (dysgraphia), which is typically accommodated by technology, or from an organizational standpoint. Unfortunately, rather than focus on remediation, writing is often taught under the guise of the adage that "more writing makes better writers." Since explicit instruction at the sentence (syntax) level is not necessarily involved, many students write the same sentence structures over and over, without being able to produce better sentences or paragraphs. The following writing strategies are designed to develop an understanding of the structures of language as well as develop a self-talk strategy that can be used to upgrade written expression at the sentence level (syntax) and provide support for the overall organization of the written text.

SENTENCE-BUILDING STRATEGY (SYNTAX)

With this strategy, the student starts with a simple sentence and develops it in response to questions (oral or written) in order to build the words into a more informative, descriptive sentence. For example, the student starts with the sentence, "The dog ran." and expands it to answer the following questions:

- What did the dog look like?
- How did it run?
- Where did it go?
- What was the place where it went?
- What did the place look like?
- What happened next?

The resulting sentence may be something like the following:

The big, red, long-haired dog ran quickly to the store, which was a grocery store with big awnings and outdoor bins, and started eating the carrots that were close to the front.

WHEELS FOR WRITING

The "wheels for writing" strategy uses the wheel as a basic organizational unit for tracking details and main ideas and breaks larger tasks into smaller, more manageable units. Though many techniques such as webbing, clustering, and spidering provide visual display, the techniques do not provide the proper sequence in advance of the brainstorming. The display does not reflect the linear progression of ideas needed for an efficient advance organizer. Students who benefit from a visual, rather than a language, display typically have difficulty with sequential organization. Techniques that allow for a display that spreads sideways or in random directions do not provide sufficient structure to support sequential organization. A technique that can be used as an alternative to traditional outlining is wheels for writing, since the organizational demands are minimal and the display reflects the sequential order, supports working memory, and balances details and main ideas.

Writing is a sophisticated process involving memory, creativity, spelling, punctuation, organization, sequencing, capitalization, and word usage. To simplify the process, the wheels are used to organize the separate sections so that the work can be divided into manageable units and the processing demands can be reduced. The units can be used according to the individual's attention span, memory capacity, or schedule. The strategy supports memory (short-term and working memory) and facilitates sequential organization.

There are two main types of student writers: those who become mired in details and lack a concise, cohesive organizational framework and those who make general statements that lack details or support.

The student who includes a great deal of detail, but lacks the more conceptual organization, will benefit from using a template to establish the organizational structure before starting to write. Since the structure is set prior to the writing, the overall organization will enable the writer to stay on target, and the student will include details naturally.

The student who tends to write more global statements and typically receives comments such as "be more specific," "support your ideas," and "include details" on his or her essay answers, papers, and reports will need to plan the details in advance of the writing. For this student, a second pass using the set of wheels as a self-monitoring strategy to identify where details need to be included is recommended. The student should look at each spoke on every wheel and attach details (such as names, numbers, terms, examples) wherever possible, resulting in "visual anchors" that make sure details are included when writing the first draft.

The number of wheels depends on the assignment. The strategy that reflects the basic organization of writing is presented below; however, the number of wheels can be adjusted for use with essay questions, book reports, paragraphs, compositions, or term papers.

The student should do the following:

- Place the title at the top of a sheet of lined paper.
- Draw five oval shapes (wheels) on the first sheet. Mark the first oval with the word *Start* and the last oval with the word *End* or *Therefore*. Place a

word, phrase, or sentence in the first wheel to identify the idea or ideas that will be used to start (Introduction).

- Write one main idea to be developed inside each of the three middle wheels.
- Write a word or phrase in the last wheel marked *End* or *Therefore* to identify the ending idea or conclusion.
- Reproduce each oval on a separate sheet of paper. Around each oval, all possible details, ideas, or thoughts that are related to the idea within the wheel are attached in a spokelike fashion.
- Go back and number the ideas in the order for writing after all the ideas have been generated.

The wheels can be completed in any order. Some students prefer to fill in the middle three wheels first to support planning and identify the beginning and ending ideas.

The strategy results in a set of six pages. The first page has the five-circle overview, and the other pages have the individual wheels on them. The wheels can be used to develop an outline or to write a rough draft by simply spreading the pages out to act as an advance organizer during the brainstorming process.

The wheels provide structure to organize the ideas and information and apply a sequence before the written language is actually produced. In addition, the writing can be completed section by section without losing the organization. The wheels will display the balance of the paper (details and main ideas) and will identify redundant topics. For example, John was writing a report about his favorite rock star and placed the age of the star (17 years old) in the middle of a wheel. Immediately, he recognized that he could not generate any related details and quickly realized that he had placed a detail in the wheel rather than a main idea. He was able to self-correct the problem by moving the idea to "background" rather than having a wheel on age.

If a book report has 10 sections, 10 wheels can be produced to establish task demands and serve as an advance organizer for note taking while reading. The wheels also make sure the directions were followed and produce an advance organizer to support writing the first draft.

If only a paragraph is required, a three-wheel setup will make the structure of a paragraph visible. The topic sentence, which is a main idea, should be written in the first wheel, the body identified in the middle wheel, and the clincher sentence, another main idea, written in the third wheel. The fact that the topic and clincher sentences, which are main ideas, are written within the wheel (where only a main idea should be written) allows the structure of the paragraph to be seen in the visual display. The identification of the topic acting as the body of the paragraph provides visual support to reduce rambling from the topic since the visual prompt for the correct topic is always in view. As a student named Jenny said, "The middle wheel keeps me from starting out writing about dogs, about my uncle's dogs, and then about Orlando where my uncle lives, rather than staying focused on dogs, which was my topic."

Student Samples

Note: Each wheel should be on a separate sheet of paper.

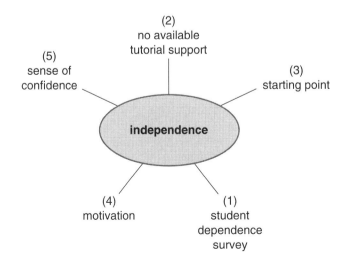

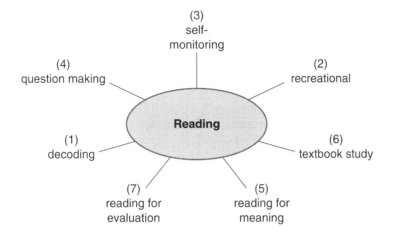

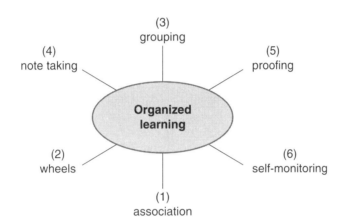

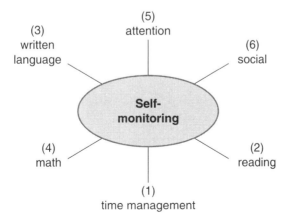

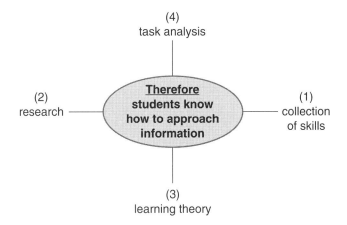

For students who need to include more details, specifics, or examples when they write, each wheel should be used as a self-monitoring tool to "anchor" details prior to writing. For example, the following wheel shows details that were added to the first wheel in the original set of wheels.

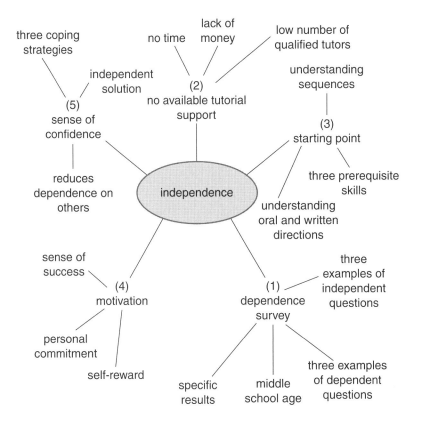

Story

A Good Guy and a Bad Guy

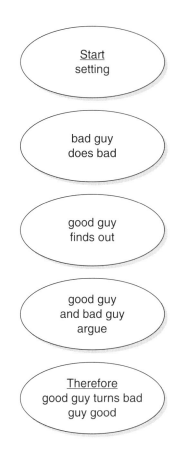

Note: Each wheel should be on a separate piece of paper.

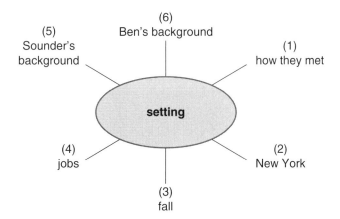

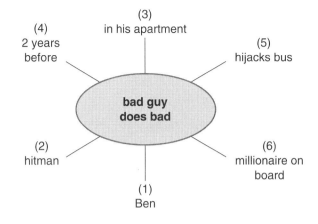

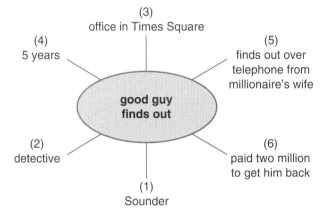

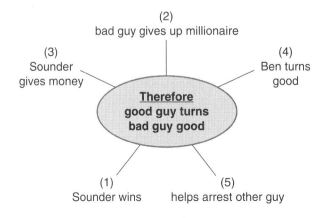

The number of wheels will vary to meet the demands of the assignment, as shown below:

- *Test essay:* one wheel, with the question in the center and ideas to be developed attached around the wheel
- *Paragraph:* three wheels, with the topic sentence in the first, the main body with attached numbered ideas in the second, and the clincher sentence in the third
- *Composition:* five wheels for the introduction, main ideas, and conclusion
- *Research paper:* five basic wheels, but for a very long paper additional sets of wheels in groups of three can be added off the three main topics to result in an introduction wheel, 12 idea wheels, and a conclusion wheel
- *Book:* number of wheels is equal to the number of chapters
- *Book report:* number of wheels matches the sections or directions required by the assignment

Paragraph

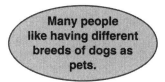

Many people like having different breeds of dogs as pets.

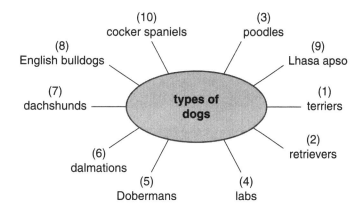

(10) cocker spaniels
(3) poodles
(8) English bulldogs
(9) Lhasa apso
(7) dachshunds
types of dogs
(1) terriers
(6) dalmations
(2) retrievers
(5) Dobermans
(4) labs

There are so many types everyone can have a favorite.

❖ ❖ ❖

Essay

Sectionalism

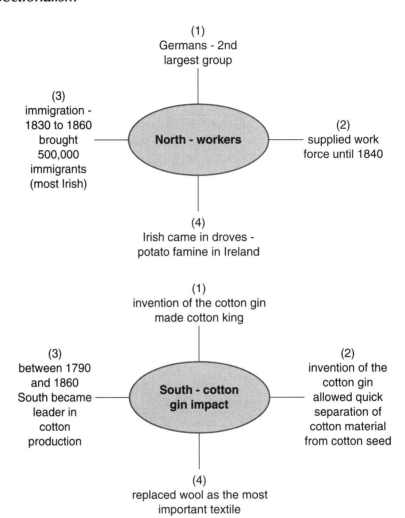

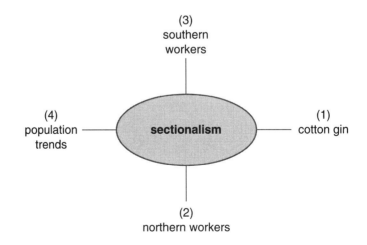

Essay during test: Write only a word or two to serve as "memory jogs" to help quickly organize the main points to be developed.

PROOFING FOR ERRORS

Proofing is a very laborious task that can be made more efficient so that the effort is worthwhile.

First, if possible, the student should proof for errors by reading the material out loud (or silently in his or her head) while using a finger or pencil to track each word as it is read to maximize attention. More support can be obtained by using a cover sheet to block the text not being proofed from view; the student should place a blank sheet of paper under the line being proofed to block out text that is not the target of attention.

After the initial proof, writing should be scanned for errors that are most likely to occur. For example, if spelling skills are strong, it is not efficient to proof for spelling. If run-on sentences are frequent, proofing should target that type of error.

To improve proofing abilities, the teacher or student (from teacher comments or loss of credit on assignments) identifies common writing errors the student makes so that proofing questions can be made out of each comment that identifies an error or weakness. The result will be a set of individualized proofing questions to be used when proofing written work. Questions are proofed one at a time to increase focus.

Student Sample

---

1. Do I have any fragments?
2. Are the verbs in the same tense?

Punctuation and spelling should be checked separately using the specific techniques listed below:

- Rules can be placed on the back of the card for quick reference. For example, the rules for comma usage can be placed on a card to use as a reference when proofing.
- Spelling should be checked by looking at each word separately starting at the end of the paper and working backward. This approach helps focus attention on the spelling of the word by eliminating the context.

A tape recorder can be used as a proofing aid in an alternate strategy. With this strategy, the student reads the text using a tape recorder. After some time has elapsed, the student listens to the tape while reading the written material. The use of a cover sheet is recommended to support focus of attention.

UPGRADE PROOFING

Though proofing is typically used to correct errors, students should learn to proof for ways they can upgrade their writing after the initial draft. Often, rewriting and editing remains an elusive concept for students, so the process must be more explicit to be efficient. When proofing for upgrades, the student should do the following:

- Look at all nouns to see if adjectives can be added.
- Look at all verbs to see if adverbs can be added.
- Add phrases and clauses to provide all the information the reader needs to know using *who, what, where, when,* or *why* questions as a self-monitoring strategy. Does the reader need to know anything else about who the subject is? What the subject is doing? Where the action is taking place? When the action is taking place? Why the action is taking place?
- Look at all nouns, verbs, adjectives, and adverbs to see if a more descriptive word can be substituted (e.g., changing *blue* to turquoise or *red* to scarlet).

This strategy provides a process to improve the writing's quality. The new draft will be more descriptive, informative, and sophisticated.

WHEELS FOR SPEECH WRITING

The wheels that were used for writing can also be used for speeches. They help organize the information, and each wheel can serve as an organizer to develop overheads, board notes, or PowerPoint presentations.

This strategy uses the wheel format as an organizational tool. When using it, the student should do the following:

- Write the topic at the top of a sheet of paper.
- Produce five wheels and write *Start* in the first wheel and *End* or *Therefore* in the last wheel.
- Put a word, phrase, or sentence that identifies the main idea of each section in each wheel. In the first wheel, the student writes the starting idea, and in the fifth wheel, the ending idea. One main idea to be developed is written in each of the middle circles.
- Copy each wheel onto a separate sheet of paper and attach related ideas around each wheel in a spokelike fashion.
- Take each wheel separately and number the ideas around the wheel according to the order of the ideas in the speech.

The resulting wheels will provide a visual outline that can be helpful in memorizing or giving a speech. The organizers can also be useful in designing index cards, overheads, visual aids, handouts, or PowerPoint slide shows, or can be changed to a list to use during the speech.

Student Example

Attention Deficit Hyperactivity Disorder

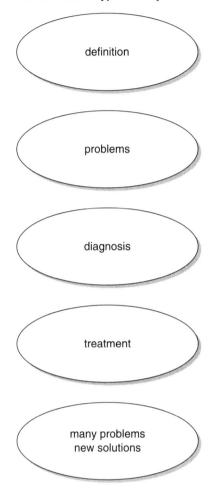

Attention

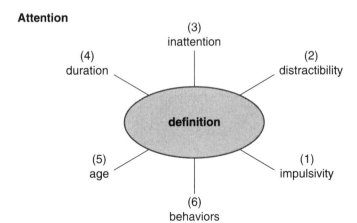

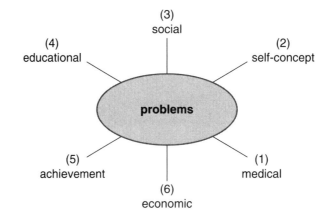

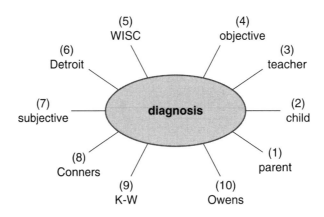

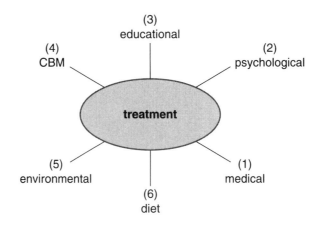

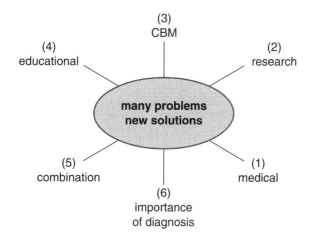

ADDITIONAL RESOURCES

Andrews, R., Torgerson, C., Beverton, S., Freeman, A., Locke, T., Low, G., et al. (2004). *The effect of grammar teaching (sentence combining) in English on 5 to 16 year olds' accuracy and quality in written composition.* University of London: EPPI-Centre, Social Science Research Unit, Institute of Education.

This article relates how "sentence combining" is an excellent, and easy, way to build an understanding of syntax to support written expression and make sentences more descriptive and elaborative.

Hughes, C. (Ed.). (2009). [Special issue on writing]. *Learning Disabilities Research to Practice, 24*(2).

In this journal, Charles Hughes invited writing researchers to summarize their research and trace its development. Articles by some of the foremost writing researchers provide rich descriptions of the systematic research on writing.

Mason, L. H., & Graham, S. (2008). Writing instruction for adolescents with learning disabilities: Programs of intervention research. *Learning Disabilities Research & Practice, 23*(2), 103–112.

This article is an excellent source to develop an understanding of the evidence-based data to improve the writing skills of secondary students with learning disabilities.

Part IV

Math and Foreign Language

13 Mathematics

Some people who have difficulty with mathematics need more verbal support incorporated into the instruction. The verbal explanation can help develop self-talk, self-instruction, and other verbal routines to support comprehension, application, and accuracy. The teacher can give the verbal instruction, and the student can record the verbal explanation to provide more support during review.

The math strategies rely heavily on verbalization, rephrasing, and application without assistance from models provided in the textbook or prompts from the teacher or tutor.

Once a student has developed conceptual understanding, it is critical for a written record to be made in the student's own words to support retention and future review. The strategies produce cumulative review systems to facilitate frequent repetition and review to develop automaticity, which is critical to be successful in math. If the student memorizes but can't apply the concepts, he or she will experience difficulty taking the test, even though the student was able to complete the homework assignments by relying on copying the models provided during the instruction.

In math, students with working-memory weaknesses, attention problems, or sequential processing deficits often have lower grades because they do not have a solid, automatic mastery of prerequisite skills or make "careless errors," even if the concept is understood. The strategies listed below support memory, attention, and retention while producing cumulative review systems. The goal is to fill in missing prerequisite skills, identify potential careless errors, and develop conceptual understanding rather than memorization.

CONCEPT, RULE, OR PROBLEM TYPE CARDS

First Card Format (Cards Made After Instruction)

For this format, the student should do the following:

- Isolate the topic, rule, or type of problem on one side of a large index card.
- Write on the back of the card a verbal explanation that explains the concept, topic, or rule to a reader who does not know anything about the topic. The rephrasing will increase intensity, develop a verbal repertoire that can be used to support application, and produce a cumulative review system.

- Have the cards reviewed for thoroughness and accuracy; prerequisite skills can be taught, and separate cards should be made on those skills.
- Review the cards frequently by recalling the explanation while looking at the concept, rule, or type of problem and then recalling the concept, rule, or type of problem while looking at the explanation.

(front of card) equation with single variable	(back of card) First-degree equations having one variable can be written in this standard form: Ax + B = C ABC = constant x = variable

Second Card Format (Cards Made as First Homework Assignment Using Math Textbook)

The information at the beginning of the section or chapter presents the concept that is being explained. The student should do the following:

- Write the new topic on the front of a large index card.
- Record any instructions, rules, or features of the topic presented in the instructional section of the textbook on the back of a large index card.
- Produce an example on the back of the card without looking at the book or notes.
- Have the example checked for errors. The errors should be highlighted and corrected and remain on the card for subsequent review.

The example should be selected from the practice exercise on the topic in the textbook. The last example in the practice exercise should be selected to force application rather than rote recall. If the more difficult example can be done correctly, the easier items will not likely be problematic.

The cards will facilitate the frequent repetition and review necessary to develop automaticity and support retention of previously learned skills that will be needed for subsequent instruction.

Math Card Sample

(front of card) average	(back of card) 1. add all the numbers 2. divide total by "number" of numbers 3. round if needed Example: 12 + 12 + 10 + 10 + 12 = 56 56 ÷ 5 = 11.2

PERSONAL REVIEW BOOK OR JOURNAL

The following organizer can be used with the instructional part of the math textbook (the part before the practice exercises) or from class notes.

The advance organizer below should be done in a review notebook (may be on a computer) or at the end of the class notes.

The following template will support topic differentiation, comprehension, and review:

Topic: The topic is often at the top of the page or section or may be in a different size or color print.

Notes: The notes are taken whenever something is being taught and should be put in the student's own words.

Example: The example should be the last one in the practice exercise.

Errors: The errors are any corrections made to the examples, any predicted errors, or any test errors.

Feature: The feature is a specific link that will help identify the topic when it is mixed with other topics.

To use the strategy, the student should do the following:

- Identify the topic (often in a different type of print at the top of the page or the section) and write it next to the word *Topic* in the organizer.
- Take notes on the instruction. The notes should be rephrased whenever possible rather than copied verbatim. The notes are taken until the instruction stops and an example is given.
- Work the most difficult example (can be the last example in the practice exercise on the topic from a textbook) in the *Example* section of the organizer. The work should be done without assistance or access to the examples in the book or notes so that reliance on the models is reduced.

If the book or notes return to more instruction, then notes are taken again by repeating the label *Notes* and rephrasing the instruction from the book until examples are given again. When examples are given, the label *Example* is repeated, the book or notes are hidden from view, and an example of what has been taught is completed (as in the second and third bullet points above).

- Predict any potential careless errors after the instruction and examples are finished (before the practice exercises begin). If none can be identified, the teacher may identify potential errors. Examples should be corrected by someone who knows the subject area (can be teacher, parent, or peer), and the corrections should be made by placing a square around the error and correcting it. The errors made on the examples should be included in the *Errors* section as potential errors. The purpose of the *Errors* section is to force awareness of possible errors and decrease the occurrence of such errors in the future. Errors that are made on quizzes, homework, class work, and tests are added to the section after the test has been returned.

- Choose a particular feature to help identify the topic in the future when it may be mixed with other topics.

There will be as many *Notes* and *Examples* sections as needed, but there will be only one *Errors* and one *Features* sections.

The organizer should be done for each topic after the topic has been taught in class.

Student Sample

Textbook Section

Mean, Median, Mode

The mean is the point in a distribution that balances all the numbers on either side of it.

Example: $4 + 3 + 6 + 7 + 10 = 30 \div 5 = 6$

The mean is very sensitive to extreme measurements when the measurements are not balanced on either side of it.

Example: $1 + 6 + 26 + 6 + 6 + 2 + 2$

$1 + 6 + 6 + 6 + 2 + 2 + 26 = 49 \div 7 = 7$

The median is the number that divides the distribution so that the same number of scores is on either side of it.

Example: 2, 6, 7, 10, 47—median is 7

The mode is the score with the greatest frequency and is determined by looking at the scores rather than by calculation. The table provides an example:

Test Scores	Frequency
100	2
95	2
90	18
85	16
80	5
75	1
70	1
below 70	1

The mode is 90.

Student Sample

Student notes made for the math textbook section above would look like this:

Topic: Mean, Median, Mode

Notes: Mean is the balance point (like an average).

Example: $2 + 6 + 8 + 4 + 10 = 30 ÷ 5 = 6$

Notes: Mean is sensitive to extremes.

Example: $1 + 2 + 3 + 48 + 4 + 2$—mean is 10

Notes: median—same number of scores on each side

Example: 8, 10, 12, 14, 18—median is 12

Notes: mode—greatest frequency—can just look at scores and identify

Example: $10 + 15 + 10 + 2 + 10 + 6 + 10$—mode is 10

Errors: mixed up median and mode; forgot to label

Feature: label of mean, median, or mode

WORD PROBLEMS

Word problems are troublesome for many people. To understand the problem, the student should do the following:

- Attack the problem "chunk by chunk."
- Make the relationship among the pieces of information visual by drawing a diagram or picture showing how the pieces of information are related.

A *chunk* may be part of a sentence, or a whole sentence, but not more than one sentence. The student should make any drawing that will help display the information, which may be confusing, visually (i.e., direction, order, or sequence). The examples that follow will show sample diagrams to depict the strategy.

Problem

Jim lent Mary $25.00. Mary gave Jane $10.00 and lent Sarah $3.00. Phyllis paid Mary the $18.00 she had borrowed, and Mrs. Adams gave Mary the $10.00 from her babysitting job. Mary wanted to pay off her debt to Jim. How much money would she have left after she paid Jim?

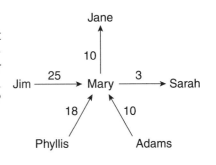

Problem

Jim owes Bill $25.00. Mary pays Jim $50.00 that she borrowed the week before. Sue borrows $30.00 from Jim. How much money can Jim pay Bill?

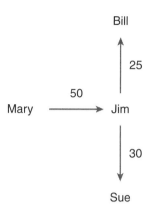

ADDITIONAL RESOURCES

Baxter, J. A. (2008). Writing in mathematics: Alternative form of discourse for academically low-achieving students. *Perspectives on Language and Literacy, 34*(2), 37–40.

This article discusses the rationale for using writing to learn mathematics, identifies the successes and challenges of using writing in math, and provides suggestions for using writing to support thinking when doing math.

Foegen, A. (2008). Algebra progress monitoring and interventions for students with learning disabilities. *Learning Disability Quarterly, 31*(2), 65–78.

This article summarizes instructional strategies with an evidence base demonstrating efficacy in improving algebra performance.

Van Garderen, D. (2007). Teaching students with LD to use diagrams to solve mathematical problems. *Journal of Learning Disabilities, 40*(6), 540–553.

This study taught eighth-grade students with LD to use diagrams to support their mathematical processing, and the results supported the use of the strategy. In addition, the students generalized the use of diagrams to other tasks.

Woodward, J. (2008). Dialogue is important: Language in mathematics classrooms [Special issue]. *Perspective on language and literacy.* Baltimore, MD: International Dyslexia Association.

This publication presents four articles that discuss mathematics from a variety of perspectives including self-talk, schema-based instruction, language of mathematics, and writing in mathematics.

14 Foreign Language

VOCABULARY

Vocabulary development is critical to foreign language study. Index cards should be made on vocabulary words when assigned so that the number of new words remains manageable and a cumulative review system is developed.

For difficult words, the student should do the following:

- Write the correct spelling of the vocabulary word on an index card while saying the letters mentally.
- Mark any visual clues such as smaller words within words by underlining the clues.
- Write the words with eyes closed to force attention on the order of the letters and accent marks (if eyes are closed, the location of the accent mark must be addressed immediately since placement would not be possible after completing the word).
- Write the word's definition on the back of the card.

The student can also produce a meaningful sentence in English that includes the foreign language word. The sentence provides additional context to support retention of the learned word and is particularly helpful with difficult to remember words.

If a word has multiple meanings, the student can make a mnemonic device by making an association using the first letter of the first word of each meaning. For example, for the French word *tenter* with the meanings *to attempt, to try,* and *to tempt,* the association is *TAT. TAT* is a memory aid to recall *try, attempt,* and *tempt.*

Student Example

(front of card)
impero
im <u>per</u> o
impero

(back of card)
Command, order, give orders, govern
c ommand
o rder
g ive orders
g overn

The cards act as a cumulative review system that can be divided into *sure* and *not sure* piles. The cards should be studied by focusing on the word to the meaning and on the meaning to the word. Column organizers can be used instead of cards if preferred.

A shorter version can be used by having the student simply write the word on one side of the card with eyes closed and write the definition on the back. A context sentence would be added only for words that are problematic.

(front of card) étudiant (written with eyes closed)	(back of card) student I am an étudiant in Mrs. Jones' second-period English class.

CHART CARDS

Chart cards use the information presented in charts in a format designed to develop a review system that makes frequent repetition and review much faster, which is critical to success in the study of a foreign language. Frequent review, however, is difficult when charts are embedded in text throughout the textbook. The information in charts should be studied until recall is automatic.

After studying the chart, the student should do the following:

- Copy the chart's outline onto a large index card.
- Complete the empty chart on the card from memory.
- Correct the chart by comparing the chart card with the chart in the book.
- Highlight errors by drawing a square around the error and correcting the mistake. The highlighted errors should remain on the cards so attention is focused on "trouble spots" during subsequent review.

CONCEPT, RULE, OR TOPIC CARDS

This simple system uses flash cards to isolate the concepts, rules, or topics on one side of an index card. The concept, rule, or topic is explained on the back of the card, and an original example is produced to support application. The card is then checked to identify and correct careless errors. The cards should be reviewed frequently to develop automaticity.

(front of card) Directed dialogue	(back of card) Conversations in which the speakers are told what to say. "Preguntele si" is used in a question and "digale que" is used for a remark. Preguntele a Susana si Maria esta en casa. Digale que si, que esta en casa.

PERSONAL GRAMMAR
REVIEW BOOK OR JOURNAL

The following organizer can be used with the instructional part of the foreign language textbook (the part before the practice exercises) or with class notes or handouts in conjunction with the strategies for building vocabulary and learning charts.

The advance organizer below should be done in a review notebook or in a computer file. The template is similar to the math and grammar strategies since all require comprehension and application as well as memorization and recall.

Topic: The topic is often at the top of the page or section or may be in a different size or color print.

Notes: The notes are taken whenever something is being taught and are put into one's own words.

Example: The example produced should be original and completed without any opportunity to see the instructional examples.

The student should do the following:

- Identify the topic (usually in a different type of print at the top of the page or section) and write it next to the word *Topic* in the organizer.
- Take notes on the instruction. Notes should be rephrased whenever possible rather than copied in a rote fashion. Notes are taken until the instruction stops and an example is given.
- Make up an example in the *Examples* section of the organizer (must close the book and produce examples *without looking at the provided examples* to reduce reliance on models that will not be available on a test). Examples should be checked for errors.

If instruction continues, then notes are taken again by repeating the label *Notes* and rephrasing the instruction until examples are given again. When examples are given, the student repeats the label *Example*, covers up the provided examples, and produces original examples.

There will be as many sections of notes and examples as the textbook has, but there will only be one topic section.

The organizer should be done on each topic presented in class or assigned for study so that the resulting notebook will support comprehension, retention, and accuracy when applying the learned concepts or rules. In addition, application of the rules or principles is forced by making original examples of what was taught in the instruction. Attention will be focused on errors that can be clarified during the study process rather than on a test or exam.

In addition to the concept or rule cards or notebook, chart and vocabulary cards should be made since mastery of all three is needed to develop command of the foreign language.

Sample Textbook Material (French)

L' = Article Defini

	Masculine	Feminine
Singular	*le (l')*	*la (l')*
Plural	*les*	*les*

Le and *La* are changed to *l'* before a word beginning with a vowel or an *h*.

Example: l'ami, l'heure

The article is like the article in English when it is used.

Example: les femmes

The article changes to agree in gender and number with the object.

Example: la terre, les villes, et les femmes

Student Sample (Done on Above Textbook Material)

Topic: L' = Article Defini

Notes: le—masculine singular

La—feminine singular

Les—masculine and feminine plural

L'—used before word beginning with a vowel or an *h*—just like in English with *a* or *an* (e.g., a friend, an hour)

Example: le—le garcon

La—la fille

Les—les enfants

L'—l'homme

Notes: like articles in English

Example: les enfants—the children

Notes: change the article to match the direct object

Example: l'homme, les enfants, et la femme

ADDITIONAL RESOURCES

Duvall, E. (2006). Including students with disabilities in foreign language class. *Teaching Exceptional Children, 38*(6), 42–48.

This article discusses strategies, tips, and advice in a very easy-to-read format for teachers who are teaching a foreign language to students with disabilities.

Sparks, R. L. (2006). Is there a "disability" for learning a foreign language? *Journal of Learning Disabilities, 39*(6), 544–557.

In this article, Sparks discusses the problems with identification of a foreign language learning disability, presents some options for identification, and emphasizes the need for special instruction to enable students to fulfill the requirement rather than use waivers or substitutions.

Sparks, R. L., Artzer, M., Patton, J., Ganschow, L., Miller, K., Hordubay, D. J., et al. (1998). Benefits of multisensory structured language instruction for at-risk foreign language learners: A comparison study of high school Spanish students. *Annals of Dyslexia, 68,* 239–270.

This study demonstrates the efficacy of using specialized instruction to support foreign language learning for at-risk students.

Part V

Test Taking

15 Test Preparation and Test Taking

Taking a test produces anxiety in everyone. For some, the level of anxiety actually helps improve performance. However, if the level of anxiety gets too high, performance deteriorates. The following strategies are simple techniques that can reduce test anxiety to appropriate levels.

IMAGERY

Imagery is used here to refer to the imagination creating a positive image that will have a calming effect. The student should imagine completing the task with a successful outcome and pleasant ending. The simple process of imagining something positive or pleasant will reduce anxiety. The example below demonstrates the use of imagery as it relates to academics.

Jeffrey had a comprehensive math examination that he had prepared for over a period of one month. There was an hour delay in the administration of the exam, and he became very nervous. When he was finally handed the examination booklet, he froze! He couldn't remember anything. Jeffrey stopped and imagined himself preparing all those weeks for the exam. Then he imagined himself taking the test, handing the test to the teacher (who had a big smile on her face), and the teacher returning the test with a very good grade. He imagined how wonderful it would feel to pass the exam and not have to worry about studying the material any more. He immediately felt relaxed rather than anxious. He took the exam and passed on the first try!

PRETEST PREPARATION

If the strategies are used consistently, review systems encompassing details and main ideas will be produced for every subject, making the review process very clear.

To organize study time, a time management schedule (see *Time Management* in Chapter 17) should be made for all the subjects and types of material that need to be reviewed. Preparation should start as soon as possible so that the memory is not overloaded by "cramming" at the last minute.

The student should make a wheel and attach the review tasks for each subject (such as reviewing old quizzes or tests) around the wheel. The student numbers each task and then counts the number of days available for studying up to the night before the test. A square should be drawn for each day available for studying. The student then distributes the tasks over the days by putting task numbers in the squares. All the tasks are distributed over the amount of days available.

GENERAL REVIEW

Index cards or two-column notes should be reviewed using retrieval practice. If using cards, they should be divided into *sure* and *not sure* piles. The *not sure* cards should be reviewed until all of the detail and main idea cards are in the *sure* pile. For the two-column format, one column should be hidden so information is retrieved from memory. Any "wheels," old quizzes or tests, or homework assignments should be reviewed. Questions at the end of the chapter should be answered orally to facilitate expression. Questions that can't be answered should be reviewed and additional notes taken on the particular topic, if necessary.

VOCABULARY REVIEW

The student should repeat vocabulary words into a tape recorder at a slow pace. Then, the tape is played back as a dictation to provide a practice test. Words that are incorrect or unknown are listed so further review can target words that were more difficult to learn.

SHORTCUT REVIEW FROM NOTES

If the streamlined note-taking method was used, a practice test is already available for review. If the two-column format was used, both columns should be reviewed by looking at the first column while recalling the information in the second column and then by looking at the second column while recalling the information in the first column.

If the student hasn't used the strategies on a consistent basis, he or she should take the class notes, handouts, or Web site printouts and use wheels (with topic inside and details attached), the two-column format, or flash cards to isolate the names, numbers, terms, or topics to make a summary of the details and main ideas, without taking additional notes. The details or main ideas that are problematic can be reviewed in greater depth prior to the test. Another approach is to make up a set of study flash cards using the names, numbers, terms, and topics to use as a practice test.

ESSAY TEST REVIEW USING
END-OF-CHAPTER QUESTIONS

For each end-of-chapter question, the student should do the following:

- Make a wheel or use an index card to put the topic of the questions in the middle of the wheel or on the front of the card.

- Attach all the details and information about the topic around the wheel or list on the back of the card.
- Number the items in the order that they will be written in an essay answer to support expression.

REVIEWING OLD TESTS

Strategy 1: The student copies the tests, "whites out" the answers, and makes multiple copies of the tests with the "hidden" answers. The student should retake the tests, correct the tests by using the original as an answer key, and make study cards on the missed items.

Strategy 2: The student makes a list of details and topics missed on quizzes or tests to identify information to be reviewed first during test preparation.

SUDDEN-DEATH REVIEW

When strategies have not been used, the review process can be somewhat overwhelming. In this case, the best procedure to use is self-questioning. The student takes the textbook, mentally turns every subtitle into a question, and answers the question into a tape recorder or out loud. Next, the student takes all the class notes, makes a list of all the topics, and explains the topics orally. It is important to express the information orally since writing will probably take too long. Topics that can't be explained should be listed for additional review.

If there is enough time, the student should do the following:

- Make study cards that simply list the names, numbers, terms, and topics from old tests and notes.
- Retrieve the information from memory using the card-sort process (*sure* and *not sure* piles) to identify areas needing additional study.

PRACTICE-TEST STRATEGIES (SCIENCE AND SOCIAL SCIENCES)

The student should apply the following strategies as a practice test:

- Fold as many pieces of paper as needed to cover all the question topics in half lengthwise and then again in half to make four squares on each side of the papers.
- Go to the review questions of each assigned section or chapter in a textbook and put the topic of each question in a square.
- Fill in the sections with the critical information needed to answer any question on the topic identified in the square without looking at the notes or text. If the information cannot be recalled, the student should locate the topic in the book or notes and list the related information under the topic in the square.

To review for the test again, the student should do the following:

- Use a cover sheet to block out the topic while looking at the related information and recall the topic from memory.
- Use a cover sheet to block out the related information while looking at the topic and recall the information from memory.

Questions at end of chapter:

1. Why was the Renaissance a product of urban society?
2. Define the term *vernacular* and explain its significance at the time of the Renaissance.
3. How did the invention of the printing press influence the Renaissance?
4. Define humanism and identify its origins.

Student Sample

Topic: Urban society	Topic: Vernacular
Florence: capital Pisa, Milan, Genoa, Venice: cities were center of change	Books in spoken language More people could read and write
Topic: Printing press	Topic: Humanism
1450 John Gutenberg More books Cheaper books	Mirandola: author of *On the Dignity of Man* Man is good God is judge, but does not interfere

PRACTICE-TEST STRATEGY FOR MATH, FOREIGN LANGUAGE, AND ENGLISH GRAMMAR

The student should count the number of topics in the notes, teacher handouts, or the textbook's table of contents that will be covered on the test and fold sheets of paper in half, and then in half again to make as many sheets as needed with four squares on each side of the paper. In each foreign language and English grammar square, the student writes the topic at the top of the square; in math, the last practice item on the topic in the textbook's review section, or an example from the class notes, is written in each square.

For foreign language or English grammar, the student produces an original example under each topic. For math, the examples are completed without any assistance. The tests easily identify topics needing additional instruction or errors prior to the test. If copies are made prior to taking the practice test, the strategy also produces a cumulative summary for exam review.

Math Example

Topic: Single-Variable Equations Example: $6 = 3 + y$ $6 - 3 = y$ $3 = y$	Topic: Double-Variable Equations Example: $10x - 2y = 20$ $-2y = 20 - 10x$ $y = -10 + x$ $y = x - 10$
Topic: Single-Variable Equations With Exponents Example: $4x^2 = 16$ $x^2 = 4$ $x = 2$	Topics Needing More Study: None Potential Errors: Mix up signs

Math Example

Topic: Variable Symbol used to stand for unknown Example: $2y = 6$	Topic: Value of the Expression Number named by numerical expression Example: $y = 3$
Topic: Simplifying the Expression Using the simplest name Example: $2y + 3y = 10$ $5y = 10$ $y = 2$	Topic: Evaluating the expression Replace variable expression with a given value and simplify the result Example: $2x + (4y - 1)$ $x = 6, y = 3$ $2(6) + (4(3) - 1) =$ $12 + 11 = 23$

English Grammar Example

Topic: Prepositional Phrases as Adverbs Example: The dog ran in the park.	Topic: Prepositional Phrases as Adjectives Example: The dog in the store was very cute.

Topic: Prepositional Phrases as Adverbs or Adjectives	Topics Needing More Study:
Example:	None
The girl in the park ran.	Potential Errors:
The girl ran in the park.	Put phrase by wrong type of word.

Foreign Language Example

Topic: Articles – vowels or h	Topic: Gender changes
Example:	Example:
L'amie est belle.	La fille est bonne.
	Le garçon est bon.
Topic: Number changes	Topics Needing More Study
Example:	Verb – être (to be)
Le garçon est bon.	Potential Errors:
Les garçons sont bons.	Forget to make verb agree with number and gender.

QUESTION STRATEGIES

Test formats are usually fairly consistent. They are generally composed of multiple choice, fill-in-the blank, short-answer, matching, true or false, and essay questions. The following strategies should be used by students according to the question type:

- *Multiple choice:* Read the stem and try to answer the question without looking at the choices. Then try to match the answer recalled with the choices available. If none of the choices match the answer recalled, try to eliminate some of the choices to find the correct answer.
- *Fill in the blank:* Read the entire question in order to understand the whole sentence or passage before trying to fill in the blank. If the answer is not clear, the student should try to put words in the blank by reading the question with the various possible answers until one makes sense.
- *Short answer:* Underline the long words to identify critical elements needed to answer the question. After the answer has been filled in, the student then rereads the question to see if the response answers all of the underlined words in the question and makes sense.
- *Matching:* Place a check by items that have already been matched, but leave the entire selection available for scanning of possible choices for each item to be matched. On matching tests, a common practice involves

crossing through the information after the item has been used. This practice is inefficient because it increases the chance of error in the remaining items if a choice has been crossed out incorrectly.

- *True or false:* Underline all of the long words in the statement. If all the parts are true, then the statement is likely true. Whenever one of the parts is *always* or *never*, the item will probably be false.
- *Essay:* Read the question and underline the long words to identify the question's demands that need to be addressed in the answer. After the answer has been written, the student should check to make sure each underlined word has been addressed in the answer. Before answering, it may be helpful to have the student draw a wheel and attach the major points to be included (often three) around it to support memory and time management when writing the essay.

TEST-TAKING VOCABULARY

Knowing the meaning of the terms used in essay questions can enable students to recognize the demands of the questions more accurately. The student should use the following list of terms often used in essay questions to support organization when answering these questions:

- *List:* After rephrasing the question into a starting statement, just line up the information in a numbered order.
- *Trace:* After rephrasing the question into a starting statement, list the main ideas or events in the development or time span.
- *Explain:* After rephrasing the question into a beginning statement, write a sufficient amount of information to enable someone to understand the topic without anything but your answer.
- *Describe:* After rephrasing the question into a beginning statement, organize the answer so that a reader can understand or visualize the topic from the answer without additional reading.
- *Discuss:* After rephrasing the question into a beginning statement, include more than one point of view in the answer. For example, a topic can be described, but then a connector such as "on the other hand" can be used to give a different point of view.
- *Compare:* After rephrasing the question into a beginning statement, the answer must tell how the topics in the question are different.
- *Analyze:* After rephrasing the question into a beginning statement, break the topic in the question down into the main ideas and details needed to understand the topic.
- *Evaluate:* After rephrasing the question into a beginning statement, give an opinion of the topic or statement in the question.
- *Define:* After starting with the word or topic in a beginning statement, give the meaning of the word or topic.
- *Justify:* After rephrasing the question into a beginning statement, make a defense, or explain the reasons for, supporting the topic or statement in question.

- *Support:* After rephrasing the question into a beginning statement, make a defense or give the reasons why the topic or statement in the question is correct.
- *Classify:* Break the information down into categories.
- *Eliminate:* Get rid of.
- *Characterize:* Give information that not only answers the question factually but also gives the reader a "picture" of the information by describing feelings, textures, or characteristics. The use of adjectives (words that describe nouns) and adverbs (words that describe verbs) are important in this type of response.
- *Argue:* After rephrasing the question into a beginning statement, give the points for and against the topic or statement in the question.
- *Identify:* Give the definition, related information, or characteristics of the topic, vocabulary word, name, number, or term so that the reader will be able to understand, recognize, or know the importance of the item.
- *Opinion:* After rephrasing the question into a beginning statement, give thoughts, reactions, or feelings about the statement or topic in question.
- *Narrate:* Tell the story of the topic in the question.
- *Portray:* Show or create a picture of the topic through descriptive, rather than just explanatory, words.
- *Clarify:* Make the topic easier to understand by identifying the main ideas and related details in a simpler, uncomplicated manner.
- *Pro and con:* Give the ideas that state the *for* position (meaning agreement) and the *against* (meaning disagreement).
- *Solve:* Work the problem to a resolution or a point that answers the question completely.
- *Reduce:* Give the answer in a simpler form.
- *Lowest term:* Give the answer in its simplest form.

AFTER-THE-TEST STRATEGY

When a test or exam is returned, it is important to review the errors so that adjustments can be made in the study process to avoid future mistakes. The student should check to see if the missed information is located somewhere in one of the study systems developed. If the student has the information, additional study time should be allowed. If the information is not found in the study system, the information should be added to the notes.

If the short-answer parts of the test that required recall of specific information or details were problematic, more detail cards should be made in preparation for the next test. If credit was lost on the essay section, more difficult subtitle questions should be made, or more details should be attached to the wheels when preparing for essay tests. If the predicted questions were too easy, the questions should be made more difficult by using the following words as question starters:

Explain	*Describe*
Compare	*Contrast*
Discuss	*Trace*

The student should look at the essay questions on the test to make up study questions that use the same question starters for use in the future. The goal is to be able to predict questions similar to the ones that will show up on the next test.

If future exams will require knowledge of the material from the test just taken, study cards should be made on the missed information to prepare for studying for the next test. If errors on the test were "careless errors" or the result of inattention, a test-taking strategy should be created for use on the next test to prevent the recurrence of the error. Some simple strategies are listed below.

The student should do the following:

- Make visual reminders (such as writing the number of steps or parts in the answer to the question) before answering to prevent overlooking or forgetting a part of the question or a step in the process.
- Underline the long words in questions before answering to help identify the demands of the question.
- Use an artificial strategy for essay answers such as the "three to one strategy," which indicates that for every statement, three examples or supporting statements must be included.
- Use a "two-step sweep" strategy for essay questions. The student records the main points or ideas to act as a base structure and goes back to each main idea to add detail to be included in the answer. The notes are just a word or two to support memory and should not involve much writing.
- Make a cumulative list of the types of careless errors made to review in the future to increase awareness of potential trouble spots and reduce errors.

ADDITIONAL RESOURCES

Firchow, N. (2009). Great schools. *Test-taking tips.* Retrieved May 29, 2009, from www.greatschools.net/cgi-bin/showarticle/2375

This article gives some simple, straightforward tips that can be shared with students to increase their skills when taking tests.

Therrien, W. J., Hughes, C., Kapelski, C., & Mokhtari, K. (2009). Effectiveness of a test-taking strategy on achievement in essay tests for students with learning disabilities. *Journal of Learning Disabilities, 42*(1), 14–23.

This study assessed the efficacy of a test-taking strategy when writing essay answers on tests. Students (seventh and eighth graders) were taught a strategy that required them to analyze the test question, outline a response, write an answer, and review the answer. The results supported the use of the test-taking strategy to improve test performance.

Part VI

Organization, Time Management, and Solving Problems

16 Organization

Understanding the concepts of authentic visual support and external organization is critical when helping students with problems related to organization, executive function, learning disabilities, or attention problems.

The authentic visual support strategy supports organization and task completion by minimizing dependence on memory. Weaknesses in immediate memory are associated with learning disabilities, executive function disorders (deficits related to organization and metacognition), and attention disorders; consequently, organizational strategies are doomed if the student has to rely on memory for the strategy to be successful. For example, telling a student to remember to take his or her textbook home really has no support if memory is a problem and will not likely be successful. Likewise, writing a note on a page inside a planner isn't visible so memory is not supported.

It is important to have reminders placed where the visual support is automatic and prompts memory rather than relying on remembering to look. For example, materials that need to be taken to school or work should be placed in a spot that cannot be overlooked (i.e., by the door used to leave the house, in the car). Notes and reminders need to be placed where they will be seen (i.e., in a clear pocket or insert on the front of a notebook rather than inside the notebook).

External organization is a process whereby structures are established that support organization without relying heavily on sequential analysis or organization. The structure provides the organizational template, with minimum dependence on step-by-step or sequential (ordered) processing. For example, using file folders is very sequential and requires a great deal of time; in contrast, using baskets or bins as "containers" to store materials without ordering them is much faster and easier. The baskets or bins are labeled, are placed in clear view (authentic visual support), and narrow the search when looking for the material. There is no organization of the materials within the basket or bin; the containers supply a structure that manages the organization of the materials. A basket or bin should be labeled and available for every type of material that needs to be organized (e.g., *math*, *science*, *history*, *English*, *Spanish*, *homework supplies*, and *soccer* may be the bins for a particular student).

Wheels for organization is a technique used to support memory when planning and organizing. The use of a wheel (oval) supports organization by providing visual "anchors" for the items or tasks to be completed, which reduces the demands on memory. Have the student simply draw an oval and place a few, brief words describing what is being organized inside the wheel and then attach the tasks to be done around the wheel. After the items have been "anchored," the tasks can be numbered in the order to be completed. The wheel can be used as a reminder, or an ordered list can be made. The nonlinear format reduces the demands on immediate memory and supports planning, prioritization, and sequential organization.

NOTEBOOK ORGANIZATION: SELF-CONTAINED NOTEBOOK

All materials and notebooks should be organized into one large three-ring or zipped binder so that it will be heavy enough to be missed if forgotten and will contain all required materials. Some students prefer to use two notebooks, one for the morning schedule and another for the afternoon. A plastic pouch pencil case can be inserted to hold supplies such as pencils, pens, erasers, compass, or protractor. Pocket inserts can be added to store handouts or returned tests.

The folders should also have a clear plastic cover on the front and back, allowing for inserts to be placed on the front and back of the notebook. Individual class notebooks or loose-leaf paper with labeled dividers can be placed in the binder, but the front of the notebook is reserved for authentic visual support. Homework that needs to be turned in or reminders about responsibilities for that particular day can be placed in the clear pocket. The student will be reminded by seeing the material, which prompts him or her to hand in the work or fulfill the responsibility.

The front of the notebook becomes the "short-term" memory support and the back becomes the "long-term" memory support. The clear insert on the cover supports memory for high priorities that day. For example, a note such as "bring back field trip permission slip," or a note about the daily homework, can be written on a sheet of paper or index card and slipped into the clear insert to be a very visible reminder. A calendar can be slipped into the back clear cover section to help monitor the week, month, or semester at a glance.

It is sometimes helpful to put something valued in the notebook to decrease its chance of being lost (e.g., a rock star photo or a favorite picture).

Notebook organization is an area that may reflect attitude rather than organization. As strategies improve performance and self-confidence increases, notebook organization may become less troublesome.

BACKPACK ORGANIZATION

Using a backpack has become standard for students, but often papers, materials, and supplies get "lost" in the bottom of the backpack. To provide additional organization within the backpack, the student should do the following:

- Buy as many $8\frac{1}{2} \times 11$ clear plastic envelopes as needed to have one envelope for each subject. Envelopes may be color coded by subject.

- Place all materials needed for a subject (i.e., notebooks, handouts, red pencil, calculator) in the appropriate envelope. The envelopes serve as subject organizers within the backpack. The plastic envelopes slide in and out of the backpack easily and serve as individual containers for each subject.

Some students may prefer an even simpler version. In that case, one colored, 8½ × 11 plastic envelope is placed in the backpack to serve as a holding compartment for all materials gathered during the day or for items that couldn't be placed in the proper spot because of a lack of time. Each night, the colored envelope should be emptied and the papers, notices, or tests should be transferred to the appropriate places.

If students are not allowed to take backpacks into classrooms, the backpack can be placed in the student's locker so that the required envelopes can be removed as needed. Students with artistic talents will enjoy "decorating" the envelopes by drawing with permanent markers, or they may want to make a computer or graphic design to insert as a "cover page" to make the use of the envelopes more to their liking.

SELF-MONITORING STRATEGIES

Self-monitoring homework charts, which track homework assignments and their completion, can be placed in the front of a notebook so that the monitoring chart can easily be seen. For example, a list of classes can be placed on a weekly sheet divided into days, and assignments can be checked off as they are completed and placed in the clear insert on the notebook. The simpler the chart, the better it may work. Often, complicated strategies are developed that do not have much chance of being successful because the demands on processing are so high.

One student of mine used nine different colored markers to color code by subject and highlight writing tasks with one color and studying with another color; the problem was that the student could not remember all the color codes, and the task took so much time that he couldn't finish his "organizer" in time.

Another student had a "sticky note" strategy that he thought was fabulous (in stark contrast to what I thought) until he sat on his notebook; he thought the "sticky notes" had disappeared until he found them on the back of his pants!

Again, the simpler the system and the more engaged the student is in the planning, the higher the chance of success. For example, a student might use the pictured chart to keep track of classes that have homework assigned to track completion.

Monday					
1	2	3	4	5	6
Tuesday					
1	2	3	4	5	6
Wednesday					
1	2	3	4	5	6
Thursday					
1	2	3	4	5	6
Friday					
1	2	3	4	5	6

Homework Monitoring Chart for Six Class Periods (Place an *x* on all classes that have assigned homework and color in when completed)

SELF-GRAPHING OF GRADES OR PERFORMANCE

A simple method of monitoring performance is to put measurements on a graph so that the performance pattern is visible. For students, the most important performance measure is classroom grades. To monitor progress in a class, make up a line graph for each subject being taken. As grades are returned, place a dot on the line for the appropriate grade where it crosses the line for the appropriate day or assignment. At the bottom of the graph, keep track of the type of assignment or test that received the grade.

As soon as three grades are plotted, place a pencil over the three dots representing the last three grades, with the eraser end at the left side of the graph. If the pencil is pointing upward, the performance is improving. If the pencil is straight and the grade level is acceptable, there is no problem. If the pencil points down, some type of action needs to be taken: strategies need to be used, additional time needs to be spent, or help is needed. If there is a sharp drop, the teacher or instructor should be consulted.

The graph can also be used to identify weak areas that might need some tutorial help. For example, if fraction tests always receive low grades, some tutorial work may be necessary to develop conceptual understanding of the concept of fractions.

The graphing strategy will make it possible to recognize when grades are dropping before it is too late to improve the grades easily. The grades graph for each class can be placed at the beginning of each subject section in the student's notebook.

See the following examples:

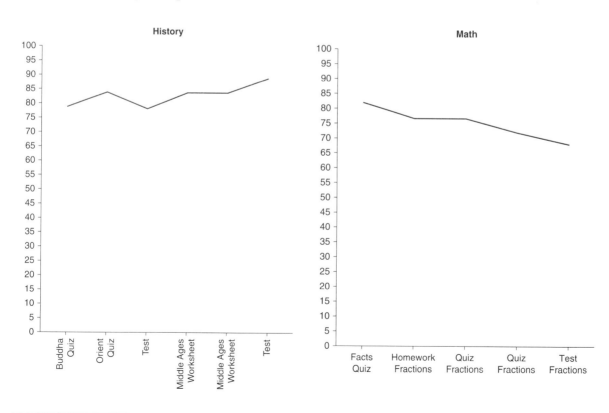

History Example   Example of Grades Needing Improvement

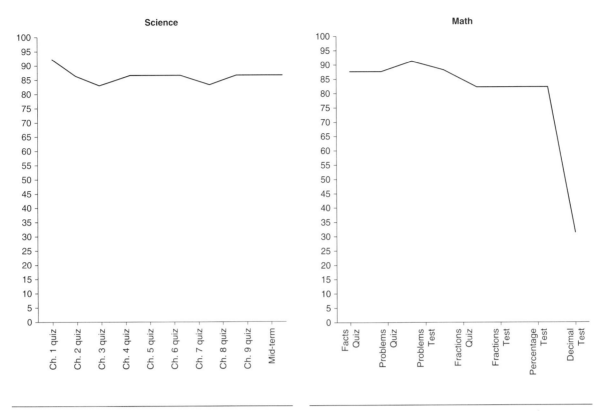

Graph of Grades Maintaining at Appropriate Levels | Graph of Grades Requiring a Teacher Conference

INDIVIDUALIZED HOMEWORK ASSIGNMENT PLANNER

To create an individualized homework assignment planner, the teacher and student should do the following:

- Make a form (advance organizer) on a sheet of paper or in a computer file (see the example that follows) that includes every typical assignment. The advance organizer should be developed with the student and reflect the actual types of assignments he or she usually gets in each class.
- Add assignments as needed. One section marked *Other* is included for more random or single-occurrence assignments.
- List *Quiz*, *Test*, and *Project* in the margin or under the subject heading to increase focus of attention through the isolation of these prompts from the assignments. Personal responsibilities (such as youth group meetings, taking out the dog, or cleaning the bedroom) can also be included.

The form prompts the student to think about possible assignments or evaluations and reduces the writing to simply filling in blanks or circling items. The forms can be kept in a separate assignment folder, made into an assignment book (can be done at copy centers), or stapled in an agenda that is required to be used.

Student Sample

| Subject | | Date: _____ |

Math:
Quiz/Test

Workbook p. _____ ex. _____
Textbook p. _____ ex. _____
Other _____

English:
Quiz/Test

Read _____ p. _____ to _____
Read _____ Chapter _____
Write _____
Other _____

History:
Quiz/Test

Read Text. p. _____ to _____
Answer Questions _____ to _____
Other _____

Science:
Quiz/Test

Read Text. p. _____ to _____
Answer Questions _____ to _____
Other _____

Health:
Quiz/Test

Read Text. p. _____ to _____
Other _____

Spanish:
Quiz/Test

Read Text. p. _____ to _____
Do exercise _____
Other _____

Reminders:

_____
_____

STRATEGIES FOR FOLLOWING DIRECTIONS

Not following directions is often a frustrating problem. Work may be accurate, but penalties for not following the directions may result, or the work may not be accepted. To avoid these situations, specific strategies such as those listed below should be developed.

Checklist Strategy

Oral directions should be written down in a checklist format as though taking notes on the directions. The oral directions then have visual support, provide a written checklist, and allow the teacher to check for accuracy, if necessary.

Question-Making Strategy

Directions that are written usually comprise several sets of sentences. The student should take each statement in the directions and reformat it into a question. Making the questions intensifies attention and supports comprehension. The questions then should be used as a self-monitoring checklist to check the accuracy of the completed work to make sure the directions were followed. For example:

Directions: Read each of the sentences below. Mark *X* if the sentence is true and *O* if the sentence is false. Pay attention to the accuracy of the statements.

1. Did I read each of the sentences?

2. Did I mark *X* for true and *O* for false?

3. Did I underline the important parts of the statement to check the accuracy of each part?

Directions: Write a short story based on the poem that was discussed in class. The characters must include the king, the messenger, and the wise men. The topic of wealth versus wisdom must be addressed. Length: Five typed pages.

1. Did I write a short story based on the class poem?

2. Did I use the king?

3. Did I use the messenger?

4. Did I use the wise men?

5. Did I write about wealth versus wisdom?

6. Is it five pages long and typed?

Wheels for Directions Strategy

If a multiple-part assignment (such as a book report) is assigned, a set of wheels can clearly identify each component of the assignment and provide an advance organizer to guide task completion. The student should make a wheel for each component of the assignment and use the resulting set of wheels as an outline for tracking the necessary steps or information needed for meeting the demands of the assignment.

For example, if the book report has nine sections, the student would set up nine wheels with the label for each section within the wheel. Notes can be taken by spiking the information around the appropriate wheel to guide note taking and task completion.

Checklist Strategy

The written directions are simply reformatted into a bullet list. Each sentence is listed as a line in the checklist with a space between each line to support attention; unnecessary words are eliminated.

ADDITIONAL RESOURCES

Hillmann, E. H. (n.d.). Improving the organizational skills of students with learning and attention problems. Retrieved from www.cec.sped.org

This short article gives advice on materials management, notebook organization, and time management and also notes the importance of modeling for good organization.

Kolberg, J., & Nadeau, K. (2002). *ADD-friendly ways to organize your life.* New York: Brunner-Routledge.

This book focuses on organizational strategies geared toward individuals with attention disorders, but the strategies can be helpful to all students needing to improve their organizational skills to manage materials and time.

17 Time Management

SUNDAY-NIGHT PLANNING OVERVIEW

To provide an overview of the upcoming week, the student should complete the following homework assignment:

- Draw seven squares on a sheet of paper or use a weekly calendar sheet.
- Divide the seven squares, representing Monday through Sunday, into 3 sections representing morning, afternoon, and evening.
- Draw an *x* through any morning, afternoon, or evening section that is not available (e.g., Monday through Friday during the day is typically not available because of being in class, and the time right after school may not be available because of sports or clubs).

The sections that do not have an *x* are the only time slots that are available during that week to complete assigned work. Often, what seems like an entire week to finish work may be reduced to a few hours on only a couple of nights. Knowing the time constraints of the week supports realistic time management planning.

HOMEWORK, ACTIVITIES, AND EXAM REVIEW FOR A SEMESTER

A simple wheel (oval) can be used to organize tasks or activities in a visual format. Any amount of time or any activity can be organized using this system. Wheels have been used to organize weeks, semesters, hours, parties, and projects. The process is very simple, and examples follow the bulleted list. The student should do the following:

- Draw an oval and describe whatever is being organized inside the wheel.
- Attach the tasks or activities as spokes around the wheel.

- Number all the items around the wheel in any order.
- Figure out how much time is available to complete the numbered items, draw a square to represent the available chunks of time, and break the square into manageable units. For example, if one week was given for the above tasks to be completed, the units of time would probably be seven one-unit days. Hours may be broken into 15-minute units or ½-hour units. Each box represents a unit of time.
- Distribute the tasks over the units of time. Deadlines and starting points to meet the deadlines are entered first so that the items that need to be completed by a specific time are scheduled before other items. The numbers or names of the tasks are written in the available units of time.
- Use the end of each unit of time as a point to monitor progress. When working with short units of time, a timer can be set to allow the work to be broken down into units for task completion as well as to see if progress is on target, falling behind, or ahead of schedule. The goal is to increase awareness of time demands for tasks.

TIME MANAGEMENT OF WEEKLY HOMEWORK

When the unit of time (one day in this case) has lapsed, the student crosses out the completed items and moves items not completed into the next unit of time, if necessary. The visual presentation of the units of time and the self-monitoring of progress allows for speeding up, slowing down, or adjusting time limits as necessary. The strategy is also designed to sharpen time estimation skills to improve time management.

If a list has already been made, the items on the list can be numbered rather than recopied around the wheel. For example, if a homework assignment sheet is already being used, the items on the sheet can be numbered and distributed over the units of time.

The following assignments are due within a week:

1. Read Chapter 10 for history test on Thursday (150 pages).

2. Do math problems 14–21 on page 28 (Tuesday).

3. Read first chapter in novel (50 pages) due on Friday.

4. Review notes for science quiz (Wednesday).

5. Complete worksheet on commas by Wednesday.

Example

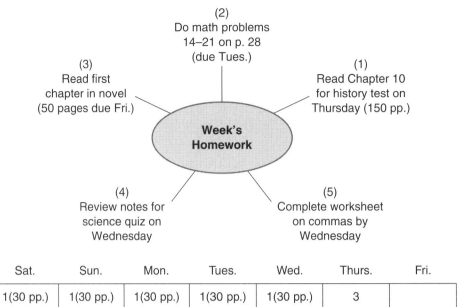

Sat.	Sun.	Mon.	Tues.	Wed.	Thurs.	Fri.
1(30 pp.)	1(30 pp.)	1(30 pp.) 2 4	1(30 pp.) 4 5	1(30 pp.)	3	

OTHER EXAMPLES

Time Management for an Activity

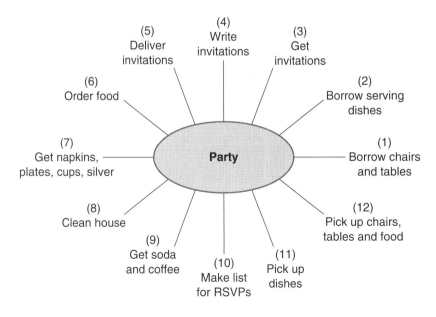

Mon.	Tues.	Wed.	Thurs.	Fri.	Sat.	Sun.
1 2 3 6	4 5	7	10	9	8	11 12

Time Management for a Week's Homework

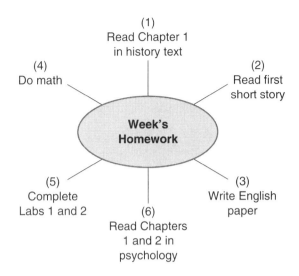

Sat.	Sun.	Mon.	Tues.	Wed.	Thurs.	Fri.
	First short story Paper Math	Lab 1 Paper	Lab 2 Paper Psych 1	History Paper	History Psych 2	

❖ ❖ ❖

Time Management for Exam Schedule

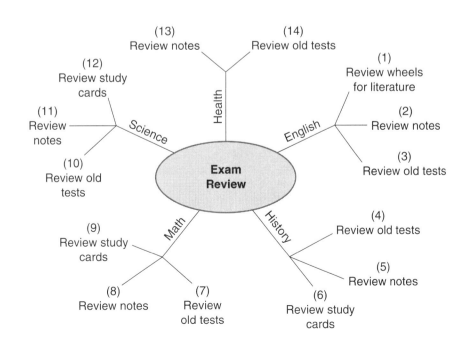

	Sun.	Mon.	Tues.	Wed.	Thurs.	Fri.
Week 1	3 4	1	2	5	6	7
Week 2	8 9	10	11	12	13	14
Week 3	1 2 3	English Exam 5	History Exam 13	Health Exam 8	Math Exam 11	Science Exam

❖ ❖ ❖

Time Management for an Hour

15 min.	15 min.	15 min.	15 min.
1 4 3	6 2 5	7	7

❖ ❖ ❖

Time Management for a Night's Homework

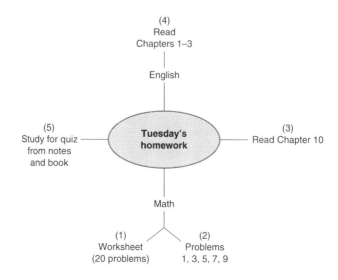

7:00–7:30	7:35–8:00	8:10–8:30	8:30–9:00	9:10–9:30	9:30–10:00
Math worksheet	Problems 1, 3, 5, 7, 9	Ch. 10	Quiz	Ch. 1 & 2	Ch. 3

❖ ❖ ❖

Time Management for a Semester (When Using a Syllabus for Each Class)

Make squares for each week in the semester and list subjects in each square. Record deadlines such as test papers, assignments, and exams first. When a deadline is recorded, back up and record a starting date the week before the deadline. Then record assigned reading for each subject every week, making adjustments for overloaded weeks. The squares represent Monday through Friday only. If the schedule is adhered to, a carefree weekend is the reward. If the schedule falls behind, the weekend serves as a safety valve to allow "catch-up" time.

Example

Key

E = English

H = History

S = Science

M = Math

P = Psychology

E H S M P	E H S M P	E H S M P	E H S M P	E H S M P
E H S M P	E H S M P	E H S M P	E H S M P	E H S M P

(Continued)

(Continued)

E H S M P	E H S M P	E H S M P	E H S M P	E H S M P
E H S M P	E H S M P	E H S M P	E H S M P	E H S M P

Example

Key

Calc = Calculus

Chem = Chemistry

M = Math

Comp = Computer Science

January Calculus Chemistry Math Computer	Calc - 1.1 - 1.3, Quiz Chem - Lab check-in M - Ch 1 Comp - Ch 1	Calc - 1.4 - 1.6, Quiz Chem - no class M - Ch 2 Comp - Ch 2, 3	Calc - 1.7 - 1.10, Quiz Chem - Exp. M - Ch 4 Comp - Ch 4
February Calc - Text 1.1, 2.1, 2.2 Chem - Exp. 2 M - Ch 5 Comp - Ch 5	Calc - 2.3 - 2.6, Quiz Chem - Exp. 3 M - Ch 5 Comp - Ch 6	Calc - 2.7 - 2.8, 4.1, Quiz Chem - Exp. 4 M - Ch 3 Comp - Ch 6	Calc - 4.2 - 4.5, Quiz Chem - Exp. 5 M - Ch 8 Comp - Exam
March Calc - 4.6, 4.8, Test Chem - Exp. 6 M - Test Comp - Ch 7	Calc - Break Chem - Break M - Ch 7 Comp - Ch 8	Calc - 4.9 - 5.2, Quiz Chem - Exp. 7 M - Ch 6 Comp - Ch 9	Calc - 5.3 - 5.6, Quiz Chem - Exp. 8, 9 M - start project, Ch 10 Comp - Ch 9
April Calc - 3.4, 6.1, Quiz Chem - Exp. 10 M - work on project, Ch 10 Comp - Ch 10	Calc - Text Chem - Exp. 11 M - Project Due Comp - Exam	Calc - 6.2 - 6.6, Quiz Chem - Exam M - Review Comp - Ch 10	Calc - 7.1 - 7.2, Quiz Chem - Review M - Review Comp - Review

ADDITIONAL RESOURCES

College Board. (n.d.). Time management tips for high school students. Retrieved from www.collegeboard.com/student/plan/college-success

This short article provides some basic advice on time management, but it also encourages students to calculate how they are spending time so they can adjust their schedules.

Newhall, P. W. (2008). Teaching time management to students with learning disabilities. Adapted from *Study skills: Research-based teaching strategies* (pp. 28–31). Prides Crossing, MA: Landmark School.

Landmark School is a well-known school for students with learning disabilities, and this article was adapted from the above book in which the Landmark staff presents its study skills program, which covers material management, time management, and study skills.

18 Problem Solving

For secondary students, the world is not just a world of academics. Solving problems, handling dilemmas, and making decisions are important to the growth and development of adolescents, but emotions can run high! These strategies provide students with a simple process to reduce emotionality, increase cognitive control, and support memory. The strategies can be used daily or on occasion by individual students or more than one student, depending on the situation. The goal of this chapter is similar to the academic applications: to give students explicit strategies to guide thinking, engage cognition, and support attention when trying to solve problems or process feelings.

WHEELS FOR PROBLEM SOLVING

If a situation is troublesome, a wheel can be used to help sort out the feelings or decide on a plan of action. The student is taught to do the following:

- Draw a wheel (oval).
- Write a few words inside the wheel about the situation that is upsetting or that needs to have some type of action taken.
- Attach all ideas, feelings, or different actions that could be taken.
- Number the ideas, feelings, or actions in the order of their importance. For example, number *1* will be the strongest feeling, number *2* the next strongest, and so on, until all the feelings have been numbered. If the wheel is being used to plan action, number the actions in the order that will provide the best results. For example, number *1* will be the action that would likely be the best plan of action.

To improve communication, ideas, details, and feelings can be tracked to take emotion out of the discussion and help a student to be more thoughtful. Two or more individuals can make up wheels on the same situation or problem so that everyone's viewpoint and solutions can be considered objectively. For example, a parent and child can each do a wheel on a problematic situation, or a teacher and student can each do a wheel on a classroom problem. An entire group can do wheels to process a problem common to the group. The problem-solving process is supported by giving visual support and forcing cognitive processing to reduce emotionality.

WHEELS FOR FEELINGS

ADDITIONAL RESOURCES

Kolb, S. M., & Stuart, S. K. (2005). Active problem solving: A model for empowerment. *Teaching Exceptional Children, 38*(2), 14–20.

This article is very user-friendly and provides a background, as well as practical advice, to help children become more engaged and active problem solvers.

Vernon, D. S., Deshler, D. D., & Schumaker, J. B. (1999). *Cooperative thinking strategy: The think strategy.* Lawrence, KS: Edge Enterprises.

This strategy portrayed in this book is part of a long, rich line of research that provides evidence for the use of explicit, learned strategies to improve student performance.

19 Conclusion

Since I have done so much instruction using these strategies over the years, I do have some concluding thoughts to share based on my experience:

- Students with learning disabilities, attention disorders, or underachievement issues often are so discouraged that they appear unmotivated. It is very difficult to separate those students "who can, but won't," from those students "who would, but can't." My solution is to teach the student one, two, or three strategies that will improve performance, give the student hope, and produce performance-improving results; if the student does not use the strategy or strategies after being shown that doing so will improve performance, the support for the student should switch to other learning supports, such as reward systems, to support motivation.

- When teaching students with learning disabilities and attention disorders, I have learned that I always know what I taught, but I do not really know what my student has processed. I always obtain an independent sample of the strategy's use or a verbal explanation that describes the purpose and process involved in using the strategy to check the student's comprehension.

- Students need to be told explicitly that the strategies should be used even if the teacher does not require their usage. For example, if the teacher assigns reading, but does not require note taking, the student should accept the fact that note taking is important for him or her and should take notes, even if not assigned.

- Students need to understand how the strategy supports learning so that they will be more likely to use the strategy. For example, if a teacher requires outlining, the student may ask to use a visual scaffold because the visual supports memory, and the scaffold establishes the sequence, making the task much easier.

- Teachers often require specific strategies, methods, or study routines in their classrooms. Most teachers will be very happy to accept a different approach if they understand how it supports learning and makes the student more successful.

- Quantity and complexity affect performance at very high levels. Some students have strong memories and do well in the early grades, but they need explicit strategies to support learning in higher grade levels as the complexity of the curriculum, the amount of information, and the expectation for independent learning increases.

- Students develop self-esteem by handling situations, developing efficient strategies, and knowing what they need to do to be successful.
- Students often equate test scores with ability level. Staying in a cycle of poor test-taking performance can discourage a student to the point that motivation becomes the primary concern. Test-taking performance should be reviewed and study strategies adjusted to improve performance for the next test. Studying longer does not always result in improved performance for many students with learning disabilities or attention disorders.
- Having students work together or in groups to produce an accurate set of study materials is often helpful to foster motivation, build confidence, and provide support for students with learning disabilities or attention disorders.
- Producing accurate review systems during the initial work is critical for students with learning disabilities or attention disorders to support learning, memory, and test preparation.

The strategies in this book have been shown to enhance learning, support attention, and guide information processing while producing cumulative review systems. Isolation, reformatting or rephrasing, and retrieval practice can improve performance in a short period of time or identify missing skills that need reteaching or additional instruction. Students will be able to work more efficiently by themselves, but can also work more easily with their teachers. A teacher can review a study system quickly, but would need a great deal of time to analyze the problem if a student comes for help with the single statement, "I don't get it." Review systems can be checked for thoroughness and accuracy without excessive demands on teacher time, can target areas needing more instruction, and can improve test-taking performance.

As teachers, we need to "level the playing field" for struggling students, including those with learning disabilities or attention disorders, who rely heavily on their teachers for help. The strategies in this book can help teachers in all settings meet the special needs of their students by teaching them "how to learn" so they can be successful in school and, eventually, in the workplace.

Resource A

How to Help Students Choose an Appropriate Strategy

To help with the application of the strategies, teach the student to use the following questions as a guide:

1. What type of assignment am I doing?

2. Is there a strategy for that type of assignment?

3. Do I need to use the whole strategy?

4. How should I use the strategy for this assignment?

Examples

Assignment	*Student Responses to Self-Monitoring Questions*
Read Chapter 10 and be prepared to answer two of the questions at the end of the chapter on a quiz tomorrow.	1. "It is a reading assignment and an essay test." 2. "I need to take notes and prepare for a test so I can use the shortcut note-taking strategy for reading textbooks and a test preparation strategy." 3. "Yes." 4. "I need to use the shortcut textbook strategy while reading so I can take notes on the correct topics and use wheels for Essay to remember the major points to put in my answer."
Read Act III and be prepared to identify quotes from the play according to the character who spoke the words.	1. "It is a literature assignment." 2. "I could use wheels for literature or the literature grid." 3. "Yes." 4. "I need to put the characters in the wheels so I can keep track of the types of personalities and actions that will help me identify the quotes."

Practice Test for Students

The following assignments were used by actual teachers as homework assignments. They were not developed to match the strategies, and assignments that are geared to a specific content area can be used instead of the ones provided. The strategies can be adjusted to meet the needs of the task. Have the student choose an efficient strategy by using the questions as a guide.

Assignment	What Type of Assignment Am I Doing?	Is There a Strategy for That Type of Assignment?	Do I Need to Do the Whole Strategy?	How Do I Use the Strategy for This Assignment?
Read Chapter 6 in your science textbook.				
Study for a quiz on Act I of *Romeo and Juliet*.				
Study for a "Wordly Wise "quiz (meaning of the words).				
Write an entry in your daily journal.				
Create a science fair project.				
Make an outline for your term paper.				
Take notes on the biographical information on Emerson.				
Summarize a news article on the debate about global warming.				
Study for vocabulary quiz.				
Write a story about a girl finding a diary from a hundred years ago.				

Resource B

List of Well-Known Literacy Remediation Programs

Alphabetic Phonics (www.ALTAread.org)

Association Method (www.usm.edu/dubard)

Basic Language Skills (www.neuhaus.org)

How to Teach Spelling (www.epsbooks.com)

Language! (www.sopriswest.com)

Lexia-Herman Method (www.Hermanmethod.com)

Lindamood Bell Programs: Seeing Stars, Lindamood Phoneme Sequencing Program (LIPS), Visualizing & Verbalizing (www.lindamoodbell.com)

Orton-Gillingham Program (www.OrtonAcademy.org)

Project Read (www.projectread.com)

Slingerland (www.slingerland.org)

Sonday System (www.SondaySystem.com)

Spalding Method (www.Spalding.org)

Spellography (www.sopriswest.com)

Starting Over (www.epsbooks.com)

Wilson (www.wilsonlanguage.com)

Resource C

List of Helpful Special Education Resources for Teachers

All About Adolescent Literacy (www.AdLit.org)

Children and Adults with ADD (CHADD) (www.chadd.org)

Council for Exceptional Children and divisions (www.cec.sped.org)

Council for Learning Disabilities (www.cldinternational.org)

Division for Learning Disabilities (www.TeachingLd.org)

Educational Resources Information Center (ERIC) (www.eric.ed.gov)

Education Week on the Web (www.edweek.org)

International Dyslexia Society (www.interdys.org)

International Reading Association (www.reading.org)

Internet Special Education Resources (www.iser.com)

LD Online (www.ldonline.com)

LD Resources (www.ldresources.org)

Learning Disability Association (LDA) of America and state chapters (www.ldanatl.org)

National Center for Learning Disabilities (www.ncld.org)

National Institute of Mental Health–ADHD (www.nimh.nih.gov/health/topics/attention-deficit)

National Institute of Mental Health–Learning Disabilities (www.ninds.nih.gov/disorders/learningdisabilities)

National Joint Committee on Learning Disabilities (www.ldonline.com/about/partners/njcld)

National Research Center on Learning Disabilities (www.nrcld.org)

National Resources for Adults with Learning Disabilities (www.nifl.gov/nifl/ld/archive/resource.htm)

NLD Line (Nonverbal Learning Disorders) (www.nldline.com)

Nonverbal Learning Disorders (NLD) (www.nlda.org)

Recordings for the Blind and Dyslexic (www.rfbd.org)

Special Education Resources on the Internet (SERI) (www.seriweb.com)

What Works Clearinghouse (www.ies.ed.gov/ncee/wwc)

Resource D

Glossary

Advance organizers   are forms or graphics that establish the task or organizational demands in advance of the processing to support thinking right from the start of the task and produce "reminders" to finish parts of the task that have not been completed.

Cards and column formats   refer to systems using flash cards (e.g., index cards) or paper folded in half lengthwise to create two columns. Some teachers refer to the latter as a "hot dog" fold. The formats provide a structure to produce review systems that use isolation, reformatting, and retrieval practice. Students can choose any one of the formats (rectangles, squares, grids, charts, cards, or two columns) based on preference. Computerized versions are also available at www.krooney.com.

Concrete guides   refer to guides, starting points, or hints that are very explicit and do not depend on judgment, prior knowledge, or reasoning. For example, looking for subtitles by searching for a different font style is a concrete guide. Looking for a capital letter to identify a name is another concrete guide.

Cover sheets   refer to the use of blank paper or cards to cover or block all information except the information that should be the target of attention. Visual distraction is reduced and focus of attention is supported.

Isolation   refers to the removal of information from text or other material so that attention is artificially targeted on the appropriate information. Surrounding the information with white space forces attention to the information and guides memory processing since no other information is available during processing.

Manipulatives   refer to specific techniques involving motor activity, such as making notations or card sorting, to help sustain attention, increase intensity, and support processing.

Multisensory processing   refers to an approach that integrates visual, auditory, and tactile processing through seeing the material (visual), using self-talk (auditory), and writing or sorting (tactile).

Reformatting or rephrasing   means changing the information to a new format or having the student explain the information verbally or in writing. The goal is to reduce rote memorization and "busy work" that does not engage the student's thinking. Information should always be reformatted (such as changing standard textbook paragraphs into lists or literature text into charts) or put into the student's own words.

Retrieval practice   requires the student to recall information from memory without support. The use of index cards or two-column formats produces retrieval practice systems, since the names, numbers, terms, and topics are isolated on the front of the card or first column, and the related information is hidden from view on the back of the card or second column.

Review systems   refer to the production of some type of summary of the critical information at the time of the initial processing to support retention.

Squares, grids, or charts   refer to visual organizers that are more categorical and are used to organize information to focus attention, to highlight details and main ideas, and to clearly identify concepts. Rectangles, squares, charts, or grids are made by folding a sheet of paper in half lengthwise and then folding again to produce four squares. The sections are labeled by category, and notes are taken within each section as appropriate. If more than four sections are needed, a second page is made so that the categories can all be seen while the work is being done. The only time information is placed on the back of the sheet is when the room in any of the sections is not large enough.

Visual anchors   refer to supports for memory problems such as short-term memory or working memory (the ability to manipulate information in memory without visual support) deficits. The visual anchors are simply information that is written down immediately to "anchor" the information and bypass memory during subsequent processing.

Wheels   refer to ovals that support processing by separating information into details and main ideas in a visual display. The wheel is simply an oval with the main idea or concept written within the wheel (oval), and the details or related information spiked around the outside of the wheel. Wheels differ from mindmapping, webbing, spidering, or clustering because the format is always linear (one wheel placed underneath the previous wheel) and will never branch out sideways. The linear format organizes the sequence visually to display the order of the task's demands or establishes a logical progression of ideas rather than a more scattered array of ideas.

Index

CORWIN

A SAGE Company

The Corwin logo—a raven striding across an open book—represents the union of courage and learning. Corwin is committed to improving education for all learners by publishing books and other professional development resources for those serving the field of PreK–12 education. By providing practical, hands-on materials, Corwin continues to carry out the promise of its motto: **"Helping Educators Do Their Work Better."**